Main Residence Relief

2nd edition

Ximena Montes Manzano

Disclaimer

This publication is sold with the understanding that neither the publishers nor the authors, with regard to this publication, are engaged in providing legal or professional services.

The material contained in this publication does not constitute tax advice and readers are advised that they should always obtain such professional advice before acting, or refraining from acting, on any information contained in this book. Readers are also advised that UK tax law is subject to frequent and unpredictable change.

Every effort has been taken to compile the contents of this book accurately and carefully. However, neither the publisher nor the author can accept any responsibility or liability to any person, whether a purchaser of this book or not, in respect of anything done or omitted to be done by any such person in reliance, partly or wholly, on any part or on the whole of the contents of this book.

Law date

The text is based on the tax law as at 3 April 2018.

First edition September 2015
This edition May 2018

Main Residence Relief

2nd edition

Ximena Montes Manzano

Published by:

Claritax Books Ltd
6 Grosvenor Park Road
Chester, CH1 1QQ

www.claritaxbooks.com

ISBN: 978-1-912386-08-6

Other titles from Claritax Books

Other titles from Claritax Books include:

- A-Z of Plant & Machinery
- Advising British Expats
- Capital Allowances
- Construction Industry Scheme
- Discovery Assessments
- Employee Benefits & Expenses
- Employment Status
- Entrepreneurs' Relief
- Enterprise Investment Scheme
- Financial Planning with Trusts
- Furnished Holiday Lettings
- Pension Tax Guide
- Research & Development
- Residence: The Definition in Practice
- Stamp Duty Land Tax
- Tax Chamber Hearings
- Tax Losses
- VAT Registration

See www.claritaxbooks.com for details of further titles due for publication in the coming months.

To my husband Rafael, for his unwavering belief in me.

About the author

Ximena Montes Manzano, BSc, Barrister-at-law specialises in all areas of taxation and practises from Temple Tax Chambers in London. Ximena provides advice, litigation support and advocacy services in the tax tribunals and higher courts to accountants, tax advisers and lawyers.

Ximena has experience of capital gains tax and in particular main residence relief and has successfully represented and defended her clients' entitlement to that relief in circumstances where HMRC had misunderstood the salient facts of the case and/or the legal tests. She is a regular contributor to the professional press, a technical editor, an author of text books and counsel instructed by the professional bodies' working party on Professional Conduct to review and advise on the guidance *Professional Conduct in Relation to Taxation.*

Ximena was the 2014 winner of the *Rising Star* category at the *Taxation* awards.

About the publisher

Claritax Books publishes specialist tax titles, complementing what is on offer from the larger tax publishers. Typically, our books cover niche topics in greater depth or take a more practical approach to particular tax issues. Our titles are written for accountants (both in-house and in practice), tax advisers, employers, lawyers and other professionals. Our authors include barristers, solicitors, accountants and other experienced tax specialists.

Claritax Books titles cover (among other topics) tax appeals, capital allowances, the statutory residence rules, CGT reliefs, the CIS scheme, pensions and trusts, stamp duty land tax, VAT, employment taxes and furnished holiday lettings. Visit www.claritaxbooks.com for details of all our books.

Claritax Books is a trading name of Claritax Books Ltd (company number 07658388, VAT number 114 9371 20). The company is based in Chester, England.

Abbreviations

Art.	Article
BTC	British Tax Cases
CA	Capital allowances manual
CG	Capital gains manual
CGT	Capital gains tax
CGTA 1979	Capital Gains Tax Act 1979
Ch	Chapter
CIR	Commissioners of Inland Revenue
CPO	Compulsory purchase order
CTA 2009	Corporation Tax Act 2009
EGCS	Estates Gazette Case Summaries
EIM	Employment income manual
ESC	Extra statutory concession
EWCA	England and Wales Court of Appeal
FA	Finance Act
FB	Finance Bill
FHL	Furnished holiday letting
GAAR	General anti-abuse rule
HMIT	HM Inspector of Taxes
HMRC	HM Revenue & Customs
ICTA 1970	Income and Corporation Taxes Act 1970
IHT	Inheritance tax
ITA 2007	Income Tax Act 2007
ITEPA 2003	Income Tax (Earnings and Pensions) Act 2003
ITTOIA 2005	Income Tax (Trading and Other Income) Act 2005
NRCGT	Non-resident capital gains tax
Pt.	Part
RNRB	Residence nil rate band
RPI	Residential property interest
S.	Section
Sch.	Schedule
SI	Statutory instrument
SP	Statement of Practice
SpC	Special Commissioners
TC	Tax Chamber
TCGA 1992	Taxation of Chargeable Gains Act 1992
TIOPA 2010	Taxation (International and Other Provisions) Act 2010
TMA 1970	Taxes Management Act 1970
UKFTT	United Kingdom First-Tier Tribunal
UKUT	United Kingdom Upper Tribunal
VATA 1994	Value Added Tax Act 1994

Table of contents

1. Historical overview

1.1 The spirit of the legislation on capital gains tax

A new tax on capital gains was introduced (alongside a specialised tax on companies' profits – corporation tax) by the Labour Government in FA 1965. The then Financial Secretary to the Treasury, Mr. Niall MacDermot, explained to the House of Commons during the Second Reading of the Finance (No. 2) Bill 1965 that:

> "I do not think that I need deal at great length with this. The general purpose of this tax is well understood, and I think accepted. It is to tax substantial sources of revenue which have hitherto escaped the tax net and so to remove an obvious social injustice and one which has been a major obstacle to achieving an incomes policy. It will also discourage or render less profitable many avoidance devices aimed at dressing up as capital what is essentially income."

Despite the obvious legitimate aim of the new tax on capital, even Mr MacDermot recognised that not all of an individual's capital assets should be subject to the new tax and, in the same breath, added:

> "Firstly, may I remind the House of the assets that will not be subject to charge. The tax will not apply to a person's only or main residence … "

Blissfully unaware of what the future held, members (in particular Mr Edward Heath (Bexley)) of the House complained about the length and complexity of the Bill:

> "Our first task … is to comprehend the Finance Bill in its present form. It might be easier to comprehend were we not so apprehensive about what we might apprehend if we had comprehended it. It is the longest and most complicated Finance Bill for over 50 years.
>
> I must offer a protest against so much legislation by reference in a Bill which makes fundamental changes of this kind. It places an intolerable burden on hon. Members. I see that even the chartered accountants, according to *The Times*, have declared that this is the last straw.

... Everybody will agree by this time that any idea that this has led to a simplification of the tax system is way out through the window."

Another 50 years have passed and we are further still from a simplified tax system. Capital gains tax has significantly expanded and continues to evolve with different rules for securities and companies, businesses, settled property and land as well as an extensive range of exemptions and reliefs. Despite the ever-changing landscape of this tax, main residence relief has managed to stay relatively unaffected since its inclusion in the *Capital Gains Tax Act* 1979. Notwithstanding the above, FA 2014 presented the first significant changes to the relief for over two decades with further substantial changes introduced by FA 2015.

Another sign of the time in which CGT was introduced was the extensive debate about the 1965 Bill which paid close attention to almost every clause and draft schedule, but the main focus of Parliament's consideration was noticeably corporation tax. Capital gains tax and in particular main residence relief were at times controversial but not that controversial. The most probable reason for the lack of resistance from Members of Parliament is that the concept of an exemption from tax for an individual's most prized asset – his home – had already been introduced two years earlier.

Hansard debates: *Finance (No. 2) Bill* 1965: 2R, [712] 47, 64

1.2 The evolution of capital gains tax and "private residences"

1.2.1 FA 1962

The introduction of an exemption from capital gains tax ("CGT") for a gain realised from the disposal of an individual's home had its inception in FA 1962. FA 1962, Chap. II "Charge on Gains from Acquisition and Disposal of Assets" added Case VII to Schedule D. Case VII came into effect in order to extend the field of income tax to certain "short-term" capital gains which had eluded tax in the past (surtax for individuals and profits tax in the case of a company) with emphasis on transactions in land and securities. Notwithstanding the desire to extend the field of tax, the Government's pledge was that that this new Case should not and would not extend to chattels, owner-occupied dwellings or business assets. FA 1962, s. 11(3) and

(7) contain – in almost identical terms – the exemption from chargeable assets for "the dwelling-house or part of a dwelling-house which is an individual's only or main residence".

The exemption contained restrictions on areas used or enjoyed as gardens or grounds, on the total permitted area (one acre or such larger area as the Commissioners may allow) and on acquiring a dwelling wholly or partly for the purpose of realising a gain from its disposal.

One interesting point to note is that, at this stage of the legislative process, the words "private residences" did not feature at all.

1.2.2   FA 1965

The principles behind FA 1962, s. 11(3) and (7) were meticulously conveyed to the CGT rules in FA 1965, s. 29 which came into effect from 6 April 1965. In fact, s. 29(1) repeated the words contained in FA 1962, s. 11(3) and added a few words at the end.

Subsections (2) to (12) were virtually all new and introduced the rules on periods of ownership, periods of absences, exclusive business use of part of a dwelling, adjustment of relief in cases of reconstruction, the main residence election, main residence relief for married couples, settled property, dependent relatives, the restriction on acquiring a residence for the purpose of realising a gain and allowing apportionments whenever necessary. Despite its origins in FA 1962, section 29 of FA 1965 appeared with the new heading "Private Residences".

1.2.3   CGTA 1979

The rules on CGT in FA 1965, Chap. III and subsequent Finance Acts were consolidated in the *Capital Gains Tax Act* 1979. As its name suggests, this Act concentrated on CGT as applicable to individuals, partnerships and trustees. The rules on corporation tax and income tax were (at the time) left in ICTA 1970.

The rules on main residence relief remained virtually the same in the *Capital Gains Tax Act* 1979. CGTA 1979, s. 101 dealt with the principle of relief from CGT on disposals of private residences and the conditions applicable. Section 102 dealt with the amount of relief including periods of deemed occupation and allowable periods of absence. Section 103 dealt with further provision on the

3

amount of relief including adjustments for business use and the restriction on acquisition of a dwelling for the purpose of realising a gain. Section 104 provided relief for a property held on trust and provided that under the terms of a settlement a beneficiary's occupation would be treated as that of the trustees. Finally, section 105 provided main residence relief in cases where a residence had been provided free of rent (or any other consideration) by an individual for the benefit of a dependent relative.

Main residence relief in CGTA 1979 was subject to amendments and minor changes in the thirteen years that followed (including FA 1991). This compilation of amendments was the basis for TCGA 1992, s. 222 to 226 in similar form and substance and the provisions remained almost intact until FA 2014 and futher substantive changes in FA 2015.

Law: FA 1962, s. 11(3), (7); FA 1965, s. 29; CGTA 1979, s. 101-105; TCGA 1992, s. 222-226

1.3 Where did the term "principal" private residence come from?

Despite numerous references in articles, commentary and textbooks to "Principal Private Residence Relief" often abbreviated to "PPR", the word "Principal" does not appear anywhere in the CGT legislation (old or new). This raises two interesting questions: where did the word come from? And is its use justifiable or supported in law?

1.3.1 Legislation

An initial search through UK tax legislation for "principal private residence" bears out references to the text of VATA 1994, Sch. 8, Group 5, Item 1. Note 13 states:

> "(13) The grant of an interest in, or in any part of—
>
> > (a)   a building designed as a dwelling or number of dwellings; or
> >
> > (b)   the site of such a building,
>
> is not within item 1 if—

(i)   the interest granted is such that the grantee is not entitled to reside in the building or part, throughout the year; or

(ii)   residence there throughout the year, or the use of the building or part as the grantee's **principal** private residence, is prevented by the terms of a covenant, statutory planning consent or similar permission."

This text was part of the original version of VATA 1994 but in the form of Note 1(7). The use of the term "principal private residence" is also repeated in secondary VAT legislation as well as in references from EU case law and opinions of the Advocate General (as early as 1992).

The other statutory use of the word "principal" appears within the *Public Trustee (Fees) Order* 2008/611 (which emerges from the *Public Trustee Act* 1906, s. 9(1)) but this Order, as its name suggests, does not deal with taxation.

1.3.2   Case law

In terms of Commissioners' decisions or Court judgments referring to the relief in those terms, the first reported reference is a case heard in 1994 (*Griffin*) (coincidentally the same year VATA 1994 came into effect) which dealt with the question of whether a taxpayer was entitled to give notice to the Revenue that a house should be treated as his main residence within any period after acquisition. There is an earlier decision which uses the phrase "principal private residence" but the question to be determined was whether the taxpayer (who was in the property developing trade) had bought a house for a trading purpose or whether it had been acquired to be occupied as his residence (*Kirkby v Hughes*).

Interestingly, the phrase seems to have been coined by the Family Division of the High Court in cases dealing with ancillary relief within divorce proceedings. The earliest report which refers to a claimant's "principal private residence" was heard in the Court of Appeal and reported in 1987. In *Maltin v Maltin* the parties disputed whether the jointly-owned marital home should be sold by the husband with half of the proceeds being transferred to the wife or whether the wife should transfer her interest in the property for a fixed sum of consideration subject to any potential CGT due. The Court held that as there was a question mark over the occupation of the house as a "principal private residence", "some risk of a claim for capital gains tax would arise on a sale of the property, and on a disposal by [the wife] of her half share in the equity".

It appears that the term "principal private residence" was taken from those judgments in the Family Division and used in respect of CGT with growing frequency after the introduction of the term in VAT legislation. In a way, the appearance of the word "principal" in VATA 1994 validated the use of the term within a tax context.

Law: VATA 1994, Sch. 8, Group 5, Item 1

Cases: *Maltin v Maltin* [1987] EWCA Civ J0731-14; *Kirkby v Hughes (HMIT)* [1992] 65 TC 532; *Griffin (Inspector of Taxes) v Craig-Harvey* (1994) 66 TC 396, [1994] BTC 3

1.4 How significant is the section heading "Relief on disposal of private residence"?

Does the section header provide any assistance in deciphering whether this relief should be referred to as "principal private residence" relief or "main or only residence" relief?

The leading textbook *Bennion on Statutory Interpretation* explains the status of section headings in interpreting or making sense of a particular statutory provision. A heading to a section (also known as its title) is considered part of the Act as enacted and may be considered in construing the section provided due account is taken of the fact that its function is merely to serve as a brief, and therefore possibly inaccurate, guide to the content of the section. The text suggests that "the correct approach to the use of headings in interpretation was summarised by the House of Lords in *R v Montila*", as in the following passage

> "The question then is whether headings and sidenotes, although unamendable, can be considered in construing a provision in an Act of Parliament. Account must, of course, be taken of the fact that these components were included in the Bill not for debate but for ease of reference. This indicates that less weight can be attached to them than to the parts of the Act that are open for consideration and debate in Parliament. But it is another matter to be required by a rule of law to

disregard them altogether. One cannot ignore the fact that the headings and sidenotes are included on the face of the Bill throughout its passage through the legislature. They are there for guidance. They provide the context for an examination of those parts of the Bill that are open for debate. Subject, of course, to the fact that they are unamendable, they ought to be open to consideration as part of the enactment when it reaches the statute book."

In this particular case the phrase *Relief on disposal of private residence* appears only in the title to TCGA 1992, s. 222 and nowhere else, the words *private residence* appear in six of eleven section headers and the word *principal* is completely absent. Conversely, the term *only or main residence* appears in the body of almost every section of this part of TCGA 1992. According to *Bennion* a section heading bears less "weight" than the substantive wording of the section or provision and therefore *only or main residence relief* is likely to be a more accurate description of the relief as was envisaged by Parliament.

On balance, in terms of the second question (posed in **1.3** above) on whether there is support in law for the use of the term "principal private residence" the more likely answer is yes, there is support from European jurisprudence and VAT legislation but not from CGT legislation itself.

For the purposes of this text, and in order to follow the terminology used in the body of the relevant provisions, the relief will be referred to as "main residence relief".

Law: TCGA 1992, s. 222
Case: *R v Montila* [2004] UKHL 50 at [34]
Guidance: *Bennion on Statutory Interpretation*, Francis Bennion, 7th edition, 2017

2. Residence in context

2.1 Private residences

One of the most obvious requirements for eligibility for main residence relief on the disposal of an individual's home is the need for that home to be the individual's "residence". TCGA 1992, s. 222 introduces this requirement thus:

222. Relief on disposal of private residence

(1) This section applies to a gain accruing to an individual so far as attributable to the disposal of, or of an interest in—

    (a) a dwelling-house or part of a dwelling-house which is, or has at any time in his period of ownership been, his **only or main residence**, ...

2.2 Meaning of residence for tax purposes

2.2.1 No defined meaning

The word "residence" does not have a defined meaning in the interpretation section of TCGA 1992 (s. 288), anywhere else in TCGA 1992, or in any of the Taxes Acts. HMRC have not issued (or attempted to issue) guidance or a manual defining or explaining what is meant by "residence". The courts have also held throughout the years that it is not possible to frame a definition for this term (*Levene*) and therefore the word should be construed within a tax context to bear its natural and ordinary meaning. This lack of statutory definition also means that the question is ultimately one of fact and that common sense must ultimately be used by the decision-maker.

In the Oxford Dictionary the word "reside" is defined as:

> "to dwell permanently or for a considerable time, to have one's settled or usual abode, to live in or at a particular place".

2.2.2 HMRC's view

HMRC state that an individual's "residence" does not have a statutory definition and refer to it as "the dwelling in which that person habitually lives: in other words, his or her home".

This is a rather unhelpful definition since to the ordinary taxpayer reading HMRC's guidance, the expression "home" may unavoidably include "holiday home", "country home" or "second home". This would undoubtedly create uncertainty and confusion where the taxpayer's residence may not necessarily be the same as what he considers his home.

Guidance: CG 64427

2.2.3   Ordinary meaning / settled living place

The dictionary definition of "reside" was adopted by Viscount Cave in *Levene* (decided in 1928) and it has ever since been endorsed and used by other courts in cases spanning many years.

One helpful example is the non-tax case of *Fox v Stirk* where in deciding where a university student was resident for the right to be on the electoral register, Lord Widgery summarised "residence" as a place:

- where a man for the time being lives and has his home;
- where he is based and continues to live;
- where he sleeps and shelters;
- that is something other than short and temporary accommodation;
- where there is some assumption of permanence and some degree/expectation of continuity.

In a similar vein, in one of the leading cases on main residence relief, *Goodwin v Curtis*, Millet LJ referring to *Levene* concurred that mere physical presence in a particular place does not necessarily amount to residence in that place where, for instance, the person's physical presence is a temporary measure, a stop-gap or an inevitable consequence of his circumstances.

Cases: *Levene v IR Commrs* [1928] AC 217; *Fox v Stirk and Bristol Electoral Registration Officer* (1970) 2 QB 463; *Goodwin v Curtis (HM Inspector of Taxes)* [1998] BTC 176

2.3   Cases on the meaning of "residence"

2.3.1   *Goodwin – permanence, continuity and expectation of continuity*

One of the most widely cited cases on main residence relief is *Goodwin v Curtis*. In that case, a company known as Sandloan Limited, entered into a contract for the purchase of a nine-bedroom farmhouse in September 1983. The taxpayer, who was a property dealer, was one of the company's shareholders. On 21 September of the same year, the taxpayer exchanged contracts for the purchase of the farmhouse from the company with a view to occupying it with his family as his home. In the interim the taxpayer lived with his family at another property elsewhere.

In the same month, before completion took place and before the taxpayer had moved into the house, the taxpayer instructed two estate agents to advertise the farmhouse for sale. Completion of the sale took place on 1 April 1985 and, in an unfortunate turn of events, on the same date the taxpayer separated from his wife and moved into the new house alone. He lived there for the entire week and used existing furniture he owned or acquired from the previous owner of the house. The farmhouse was actively marketed during the taxpayer's entire occupation, a purchaser was found and a simultaneous exchange of contracts and completion was effected on 3 May 1985 (just over a month after he moved in). Mr Goodwin's case was also complicated by the fact that three days after he moved into the farmhouse he completed on another house on which he had exchanged contracts earlier and he treated this house as his residence in the 1985-86 tax return. He moved into this property immediately after the farmhouse sold and had no other properties to occupy after that.

The issue for the General Commissioners to determine was whether the farmhouse was the taxpayer's only or main residence during the period he occupied it (nearly five weeks). In other words, did his occupation amount to "residence"?

The Revenue argued that the relief was available only when an individual owned a dwelling-house which was, or had at any time during the period of actual ownership, been his only or main residence. It was insufficient simply to own the property; the relief required some degree of permanence and continuity, as well as some expectation of continuity, to turn mere occupation into residence. This taxpayer had not lived in the farmhouse with his family and used it as a temporary stop gap measure once he separated from them. This was evidenced by the fact that the house was put on the market before he moved in.

The taxpayer denied the Revenue's contentions, arguing that when he acquired an interest in each property (the farmhouse and his current house) he had intended each one of them to be a permanent residence.

The General Commissioners agreed with HMRC – and on appeal the High Court confirmed – that the short-lived occupation of the house did not amount to residence for the purposes of the legislation. Unhappy with both judgments, the taxpayer appealed onwards to the Court of Appeal. After citing *Levene*, the Court of Appeal dismissed the appeal and decided that there had been no misdirection of law by the Commissioners and that there was plenty of evidence to come to the conclusion that the nature, quality, length and circumstances of the taxpayer's occupation of the farmhouse did not amount to residence within the meaning of CGTA 1979 and that "temporary occupation at an address does not make a man resident there".

Case: *Goodwin v Curtis (HM Inspector of Taxes)* [1998] BTC 176

2.3.2   Favell – seven months' residence may be enough in the circumstances of some cases

In *Favell*, the appellant claimed main residence relief and lettings relief on a two-bedroom flat which he disposed of in June 2003. Whether or not he was entitled to the relief turned on whether he had occupied the said property as his main residence for the ten months from January to November 2001.

In evidence under oath Mr Favell alleged that when he bought the property in 1999, he planned to purchase it for his son but that the property had to be updated and renovated. Following this work the property was let. In January 2001, following his split from his long-term partner, he left his other property (which he shared with his ex-partner) and moved into the flat in question. He alleged that he lived in the property for the following ten months after which he moved back to his other property and reconciled with his partner whom he then married. The flat had been re-let after these events.

The appellant did not have any documentary evidence to support his allegations and said that he had destroyed them because he did not expect to have to prove his residence there. He had not notified any official body of his move and had no utility bills, etc. showing that address. The evidence adduced to support the appellant's contentions merely consisted of three short letters from former tenants, one of which was contradicted by evidence presented by HMRC from the local Council's Housing Benefit department which stated that housing benefit had been paid in respect of another person for the property during months in which the appellant claimed he was residing there (August to November 2001).

The Tribunal held that if there had been sufficient evidence to prove residence at the property for seven months, they "would have been minded to hold that such occupation would have amounted to residence for the purposes of s. 222 TCGA". In this case, as the Tribunal plainly disbelieved the appellant's contentions (unsupported by evidence), the issue did not have to be adjudicated upon. The Tribunal noted that the facts of *Goodwin* were "extreme" and that there had been no indication that the breakdown of Mr Favell's relationship was likely to be temporary.

The FTT accepted in *Dutton-Forshaw* (decided on 18 September 2015) that occupation of just seven weeks can amount to residence in certain circumstances. See **2.3.9** below.

Case: *Favell v HMRC* [2010] UKFTT 360 (TC)

2.3.3   Regan – quality of occupation versus quantity

The appellant, Mr Regan, and his wife bought a property ("95 Rowan") from their son in May 2000 and lived there together until June 2003. In September 2002, the Regans purchased another property ("Woodland"), financed with a mortgage which helped fund the initial purchase but also substantial refurbishment work which took two years to complete.

In February 2003, Mr and Mrs Regan sold 95 Rowan (which was demolished to make room for improvements to a club located at the back of the property and managed by their son) and bought the property next door ("93 Rowan"). Before moving to 93 Rowan, the

Regans carried out modernising works in order to make it habitable (new kitchen and bathroom, central heating and double glazing, decoration and new carpets). The appellants moved into 93 Rowan in June 2003 and remained there until April 2004 when they moved into their Woodland property. After leaving 93 Rowan, the appellants added an extension to it and eventually sold it on 29 August 2006.

HMRC contended that this disposal was a venture in the nature of a trade or alternatively, if treated as a capital transaction, not qualifying for relief as it was not Mr and Mrs Regan's only or main residence.

The Tribunal held that the need for permanence or continuity should not be overstated and that residence was a matter of fact that should be determined by reference to the quality and not merely the length of the occupation.

On the facts, the Tribunal found that even though the appellants intended to move in to Woodland as soon as it was ready, this intention did not disqualify 93 Rowan from being a residence; the property was more than a "stop gap" or temporary place of occupation. Main residence relief was therefore available for the entire period of ownership.

Case: *Regan v HMRC* [2012] UKFTT 569 (TC)

2.3.4 Morgan – intention is king

This was a rather unfortunate case which seems to have tugged at the Tribunal's heart strings. At the relevant time, Mr Morgan worked as a supervisor for Safeways supermarkets and, during time in a new location, he met his girlfriend of five years and later fiancée, Miss Varley. The couple planned to purchase and move into a marital home and Mr Morgan arranged to buy the property in early 2001. A mortgage was agreed in Mr Morgan's sole name but with a note on the deeds that read: "Special Conditions – Non-Borrowing Occupiers". The note stated: "We believe that the persons(s) named below may live at the property ... . Miss Paula Emma Lucy Varley". Miss Varley agreed to pay £5,000 towards the cost of the property.

After contracts had been exchanged but before completion (on or around 1 June 2001), and for reasons unknown to Mr Morgan, Miss

Varley broke off the engagement (it later transpired that she had been seeing someone else). Mr Morgan completed the purchase of the house on 15 June 2001 and moved in alone. Mr Morgan moved out of the property on 30 August 2001 when it was let in full and the mortgage was changed to a buy-to-let agreement.

HMRC accepted that Mr Morgan had lived at the property but argued that the fact that he had given conflicting accounts of whether Miss Varley had ever lived at the property, that he had contacted the mortgagee requesting a "tenancy pack" very soon after he had moved, and that he had "minimal furnishings" at the house pointed to the property being used as temporary accommodation. The Tribunal found the "case to be extremely finely balanced", found Mr Morgan to be a credible witness, and "did not think the quantity or quality of the furnishing has more than a minimal bearing on the intention of Mr Morgan at the time he moved in". After analysing *Goodwin* the Tribunal held that Mr Morgan need only show that at the time he moved into the property he intended it to be his permanent residence even if he changed his mind the following day. They were satisfied that Mr Morgan had overcome the evidential burden which lay on him to show that he intended to occupy the property as his only residence and that when he found the cost of living there was too high, he had decided to move out and let it instead. This meant that physical occupation of a property for even two months (or indeed seven weeks – see *Dutton-Forshaw* at **2.3.9** below) is, in the right circumstances, sufficient to make it a residence.

Case: *Morgan v HMRC* [2013] UKFTT 181 (TC)

2.3.5   *Bradley – intention is relevant at time of moving in*

Mrs Susan Bradley was at all relevant times married to Mr Bradley and lived in a property jointly owned with him until August 2007. Mrs Bradley also owned a semi-detached house and a small "bedsit" type flat, both of which were let to tenants.

Prior to August 2007, the relationship between the Bradleys had taken a turn for the worse and this led to Mrs Bradley moving out of the marital home and into her small flat which was vacant at that time. When an existing tenancy at her house expired in April 2008 she moved there. When she eventually moved, the house was in a poor decorative state and Mrs Bradley repainted it, repaired the kitchen and bought new appliances and fittings to make it more of a "home". Mrs Bradley explained in evidence that her intention was to separate permanently from her husband and obtain a divorce. To this end, she visited family solicitors to clarify her rights but did not file divorce papers. Mrs Bradley supported herself and continued to visit the marital home to see her youngest daughter and to collect post addressed to her there. She was suffering from depression at this time and was undergoing treatment. She told the Tribunal that she had not been functioning well and therefore had not had the presence of mind to change her address on her bank accounts or utilities. She did have proof of council tax payments for both her small flat and the semi-detached house.

Despite the alleged intention to separate permanently from her husband, there was evidence of an instruction dated 20 March 2008 from Mrs Bradley to estate agents to place the semi-detached house she then occupied on the market. The property market was poor due to the economic downturn and there were no offers from buyers. The house stayed on the market throughout Mrs Bradley's period of occupation.

In the autumn of 2008, the Bradleys reconciled and Mrs Bradley moved back to the marital home in November 2008. Mrs Bradley's property was sold in January 2009.

The Tribunal was satisfied that when Mrs Bradley had left the marital home in August 2007, her intention was to separate permanently from her husband and to divorce him after two years' separation. However, the Tribunal recognised that this fact in itself did not mean that Mrs Bradley's second house qualified for main residence relief. They had to explore whether Mrs Bradley had actually occupied the property as her only or main residence.

Due to the fact that even before Mrs Bradley had moved into her second property, she had placed it on the market, and her instructions were still in place when she reconciled with her husband, the Tribunal found that "she never intended to live permanently [there], it was only ever going to be a temporary home, and therefore it was never her residence". The Tribunal drew support for this finding from Goodwin and the First-tier Tribunal's decision in *Metcalf*.

15

It is important to note that in *Goodwin*, the taxpayer placed the farmhouse on the market because three days after he moved into it he completed on another house which he treated as his residence in the following tax year. In other words, he could not intend to live at the farmhouse, if he had already decided to reside permanently elsewhere. That was certainly not the case with Mrs Bradley and the decision seems harsh in the circumstances.

Case: *Bradley v HMRC* [2013] UKFTT 131 (TC)

2.3.6   *Moore – the state of a personal relationship may determine an individual's expectation of permanence and continuity*

Mr Piers Moore appealed against HMRC's assessment to CGT in respect of the disposal of a dwelling occupied by Mr Moore for eight months between November 2006 and July 2007. The property in question was a rental property owned by Mr Moore and which had been occupied by him as a result of a separation from his wife. The taxpayer had taken some furniture from the marital home and moved all his personal possessions to the new property. Some of the taxpayer's correspondence had continued to go to the marital home and one of his banks sent account statements to the address of Mr Moore's girlfriend (subsequent wife).

Some three to six months after moving to the property in question, Mr Moore put the property on the market and eventually sold it. There was evidence before the Tribunal showing that Mr Moore had made preparatory financial decisions as early as 1 March 2007 to gather a deposit for the purchase of his jointly-owned home with his new wife. Whilst it was accepted that the taxpayer had lived at the relevant property, it was contended by HMRC that the occupation did not have the required degree of permanence, continuity or expectation of continuity to amount to a residence.

The FTT decided that in contrast to the facts of *Goodwin v Curtis*, the taxpayer had formed a new relationship and moved to a shared home with his new partner and later wife. Whilst the property in question was suitable as a residence for Mr Moore as a single man, it was unsuitable for him, his new wife and her two sons and therefore there could be no expectation of a permanent residence there. The state of the relationship with his new wife was, in the FTT's view, the most important factor to consider. The FTT found that Mr Moore had a "serious hope or expectation" before March 2007 to buy a house and live with his new wife and her children. The movement of funds into a single bank account in February 2007, the fact that correspondence was delivered elsewhere and the lack of any bills addressed at the relevant property (apart from council tax) supported this conclusion. In the circumstances, the property in question did not amount to a residence in the absence of an expectation of continuity of occupation.

Case: *Moore v HMRC* [2013] UKFTT 433 (TC)

2.3.7 Metcalf – an immediate intention to sell militates against residence

In this case, the appellant, Mr Metcalf, claimed main residence relief on a property he had owned between 11 October 2002 and 27 March 2003. At the relevant time, the taxpayer owned three properties: "Everleigh" in Leeds, and "Landalewood" and "Westgate" in York.

During oral evidence at the Tribunal, Mr Metcalf explained that he had moved into Westgate in approximately November 2002 from Everleigh. Westgate was furnished with carpets, a fridge/freezer, a cooker, a washing machine and a bed. The appellant did not install a telephone or obtain a television licence. The apartment was fuelled by electricity only but the electricity bill presented to the Tribunal showed a particularly low level of electricity consumption over the winter months; namely £39.09 for a period of just over three months. The appellant's partner had moved into Westgate with him but after a very short period had moved out because she did not like living in York as the distance from her family was too far to travel.

In addition, the appellant told the Tribunal that he had obtained a valuation of the property a number of weeks after moving in, and although he could not recall the date he believed it was some time before Christmas of 2002, after which he placed the property on the market for sale.

There was no documentary evidence to support Mr Metcalf's claim that he had occupied Westgate as his only residence (no utility bills, no bank statements, and no council tax bills) and he had used Everleigh's address in an application for a credit card.

The Tribunal held that the oral evidence presented by the appellant, coupled with the lack of supporting evidence, pointed away from a conclusion that Westgate had been a residence. The fact that the appellant had not notified anyone of his change of address and that he had (within days or weeks of moving in) obtained a valuation with a view to selling the property meant that any occupation lacked any degree of permanence or expectation of continuity. The occupation was held to be merely temporary.

Case: *Metcalf v HMRC* [2010] UKFTT 495 (TC)
Guidance: CG 64200

2.3.8 Springthorpe – occupying a property whilst carrying out construction work does not equate to occupying it as a home

In *Springthorpe*, the appellant claimed that he had occupied a dwelling-house he purchased on 10 November 1999 as his residence while he refurbished it. The house in question was in poor condition and required extensive renovation. Whilst the work was being carried out, the appellant had the gas supply turned off, had no bathroom (although an outside toilet was available) and had no cooking facilities. In addition, the appellant was granted an exemption from Council Tax on the basis that the "alterations taking place ... render it uninhabitable".

The taxpayer submitted that although he had intended the property to be his home, the fact that he was made redundant and that his financial situation was deteriorating had forced him to consider the possibility of letting the house to lodgers or to students in May 2000. The property had been eventually let to students in July 2000.

The First-tier Tribunal (Judge Brannan) decided that although it considered it likely that the taxpayer had spent time occupying the property in the relevant period, he had not occupied it as a home for the following reasons:

- The minimal electricity bills, the lack of cooking facilities and the non-existent gas connection resulted in no hot water at the property throughout the winter months, which made it unlikely that the appellant had lived in the property for the entire period. He was likely to have stayed occasionally whilst also staying elsewhere.

- The occupation was for the purpose of renovating the property with a view to letting it rather than occupation as a home.

- The evidence adduced fell very short of discharging the burden of proof and the letters submitted by the appellant did not address the quality of the appellant's occupation of the property.

- The appellant was (at best) undecided, when doing the refurbishment work, whether to sell, let or live in the property and therefore he did not have an intention to occupy the dwelling-house with any degree of permanence or continuity.

Case: *Springthorpe v HMRC* [2010] UKFTT 582 (TC)

2.3.9   Recent cases: 2015 to 2018

Dutton-Forshaw – permanence and continuity should not be overstated

The facts of this case were complex and examined a number of properties purchased, let and sold by the taxpayer either alone or jointly with his ex-wife. The only issue to be determined by the FTT was whether or not a London flat owned by the taxpayer between 2006 and 2009, but occupied for only seven weeks from August to September 2006, amounted to a residence.

The relatively short occupation of the London flat had been brought about by the end of the taxpayer's marriage and his decision to move to London to live as a single man. The taxpayer contended that he was forced to move back to Lymington because his ex-wife was proposing to move to Spain and take his only daughter with her. Mr Dutton-Forshaw disapproved of this proposal and moved back to care for his child. The intention, the taxpayer argued, had been to make the London flat a permanent residence and the move was caused by circumstances beyond his control. The taxpayer's version of events was corroborated by his ex-wife's testimony.

The FTT considered the principles established by *Fox v Stirk* and held that "it seems clear that the question of permanence or continuity should not be overstated" in distinguishing a visitor from a resident. This analysis of the previous case law echoes that said by the FTT in *Regan* (see **2.3.3** above).

Taking a generous approach, the FTT held that despite the taxpayer building a property portfolio in London and being aware of his ex-wife's plans to move abroad, his intention was to reside at the London flat permanently. Based upon the evidence available, the FTT concluded that "the 'nature, quality, length and circumstances' of Mr Dutton-Forshaw's occupation of [the London property] did make that occupation qualify as residence".

Case: *Dutton-Forshaw v HMRC* [2015] UKFTT 478 (TC)

Kothari – the facts were inconsistent with permanence and continuity

The issue before the FTT was whether or not a rental property located in the Mayfair area of London was occupied as a residence. The parties agreed that if the property was the taxpayer's residence, there had been a valid election to treat it as his main residence.

The taxpayer had acquired a two-bedroom flat in Park Lane Place in 2004 and let it out until January 2009. It was alleged that the taxpayer, his wife and three children had moved to the flat on 19 January 2009 with the intention of making it their permanent home. The property was sold in July 2009. The FTT found that the occupation of the flat lacked the necessary degree of permanence or continuity, or the expectation of continuity of residence. In assessing permanence and continuity of occupation, the main considerations were:

- there was a one-month period of occupation by the taxpayer of the flat before it was put on the market;
- as the taxpayer had a four-bedroom house in Mill Hill which he occupied with his wife and three children, it seemed unlikely that they would move into a two-bedroom property just so that he could be near his offices (which were rented two weeks after the alleged move-in date in any event);
- substantial rental losses suggested that the taxpayer could not afford to lose £96,000 of income by moving into the flat;

- no furniture had been moved or purchased and there was no change in schooling arrangements;
- there was very little evidence of change of address provided – all the council tax bills went to the taxpayer's address in Mill Hill.

All of these facts pointed away from the flat in question being occupied with an expectation of permanence and continuity. The appeal was therefore dismissed.

Case: *Kothari v HMRC* [2016] UKFTT 127 (TC)

Andrew Oliver – a paper trail may not be sufficient proof

In another case where the taxpayer moved away to a second property following a marriage separation, the FTT had to determine whether the quality of Mr Oliver's occupation had the necessary degree of permanence and continuity.

The taxpayer had a property letting business and traded under two separate names. The FTT found that Mr Oliver's business owned between 10 and 20 properties at the relevant time.

Since 1999, Mr Oliver owned and occupied a main residence with his wife and two children. During a period of approximately two months in 2007, the couple had a trial separation which coincided with the purchase of a flat acquired jointly by the couple, subject to a buy-to-let mortgage and which required a lease extension. The taxpayer argued that due to the breakdown of his marriage he had intended to occupy the flat as a residence in early January 2007 but that he had decided to sell it due to an unexpected reconciliation on 16 March 2007. The sale of the flat completed on 12 April 2007.

The FTT noted that during the alleged period of occupation, Mr Oliver had carried out basic redecoration work and there was no evidence of furniture present in the flat. Mr Oliver adduced various items of correspondence as evidence of his intention to reside but the FTT held that they were consistent with a wish to create "a paper trail" rather than an intention to stay permanently and continuously. The use of the flat was uncertain when it was first acquired but the intention had changed to a "buy to let intention" when the lease extension negotiations were more difficult and costly than originally envisaged.

The FTT further held that Mr Oliver's wife's involvement in the purchase of the property, and the fact that most of the correspondence post-dated an offer acceptance and their reconciliation, were contrary to an intention to reside permanently.

In conclusion, Mr Oliver had used the flat as a stop-gap pending redecoration, marketing photographs and the necessary lease extension. Whilst there was some occupation of the flat, it lacked "the assumption of permanence, any degree of continuity or expectation of continuity".

This case is a helpful reminder that the existence of a correspondence trail is not of itself sufficient to prove residence if the other facts and circumstances of the case point the other way. Advisers should remind clients that having supporting documentation cannot surpass an actual intention to permanently occupy.

Case: *Oliver v HMRC* [2016] UKFTT 796 (TC)

Stephen Bailey – "quality trumps quantity"

In this case, HMRC raised a discovery assessment and a penalty in respect of a gain made by Mr Bailey on the disposal of a dwelling-house in the 2010-11 tax year. HMRC claimed that a loss of tax was caused by the taxpayer's deliberate conduct. It is possible that a series of procedural errors made by HMRC tipped the scales against them but since the FTT decided the case on its merits, the facts and findings are explored below.

The FTT heavily relied on Mr Bailey's unchallenged witness account and the Tribunal found him to be a reliable and honest witness.

At all relevant times, Mr Bailey was a divorcee who ran a successful property business. He lived in Maidstone with his children, his partner and her son (the taxpayer's partner split her time between Maidstone and another property in Feltham).

In February 2008, Mr Bailey's company acquired a new dwelling-house in Farnham (known as Richmond) with a three-month bridging loan. The taxpayer argued that his intention was always to:

- occupy Richmond as a family home;
- obtain a standard mortgage jointly with his partner;

- buy the property from his company; and
- let out his house in Maidstone.

He moved basic furniture into the new property (as the Maidstone house was to be let furnished) and moved with his children for two and a half months whilst he tried to resolve his financial situation. Mr Bailey's plans were eclipsed by the financial crisis of 2008 and he was unable to obtain a normal mortgage to purchase Richmond. In the circumstances, Mr Bailey had no choice but to obtain a buy-to-let mortgage which saved the property from repossession but which prevented him from living there. The family had to move to Farnham and Richmond was let out to a friend and his wife.

The tenant friend died in 2010 and his widow left Richmond shortly afterwards. At this point, Mr Bailey once again moved back to Richmond to carry out redecoration work and to prepare it for occupation by the whole family. After a few weeks of occupation, Mr Bailey fell into clinical depression (although there was no medical evidence available) due to the death of his friend and decided that he could not cope with living there. Redecoration works were finished and Richmond was sold in August 2010 realising a capital gain of £121,000. The gain was omitted altogether from Mr Bailey's 2010-11 return.

The FTT accepted the taxpayer's version of events with little difficulty and held that "one [sic] each occasion when Mr Bailey moved into Richmond, he intended that his residence would be on a permanent basis and that the property would be his home". On this basis, the FTT decided that although the second period of occupation had been brief (and the time before he decided to sell was even briefer) this was a case where quality of occupation trumped quantity.

In the absence of any corroborating evidence (there were no items of correspondence, bills or photographs mentioned, for instance), this decision seems at odds with other recent decisions and in particular with *Oliver* discussed above. It appears that differently-constituted tribunals place different weight on the existence of documentary evidence of occupation.

Case: *Bailey v HMRC* [2017] UKFTT 658 (TC)

2.4 Overseas residence

2.4.1 No territorial restriction of relief

> "But a man may reside in more than one place. Just as a man may have two homes – one in London and the other in the country – so he may have a home abroad and a home in the United Kingdom, and in that case he is held to reside in both places and to be chargeable with tax in this country." – *Levene*

At the time of writing, there is nothing in the CGT legislation that specifies that main or only residence relief is available only to dwelling-houses situated in the UK. In principle, an individual was able to claim the relief on a disposal of a property abroad which he – at any time of his period of ownership – had occupied as his main or only residence. This broad principle has been restricted by the introduction of the new rules on disposals of UK property interests by non-UK residents in FA 2015 (see **2.5** below).

In practice, a disposal of a property abroad would attract relief in cases where the individual has lived outside the UK for a substantial period of time and has become UK resident prior to that disposal. As long as the dwelling-house was occupied as his main residence (as defined) for part or all of his period of ownership, and the disposal of the house was effected within 18 months of the date he became UK resident, then the capital gain would not be (subject to any other periods of absence) a chargeable gain. If, however, there is a longer period of "absence" or residence in the UK, then the amount of relief will be restricted according to the normal rules.

If the individual who arrives in the UK to reside permanently is not UK domiciled, there is, of course, the possibility of escaping a capital gains tax charge on the disposal of his former residence if a claim for the remittance basis is made to cover the tax year of disposal and the proceeds of sale are not remitted to the UK.

An overseas residence is therefore likely to attract main residence relief in the limited cases of individuals domiciled in England and Wales who return after extended periods of absence overseas.

Case: *Levene v IR Commrs* [1928] AC 217

2.4.2   Double taxation relief

According to the *Taxation (International and Other Provisions) Act* 2010, s. 9(2) *Rule 1: the unilateral entitlement to credit for non-UK tax*, credit for tax paid under the law of the foreign territory, calculated by reference to any capital gain accruing in the territory and corresponding to UK CGT, is to be allowed against any capital gains tax calculated by reference to that gain. So, in general terms, if an individual pays foreign capital gains tax (or equivalent) in relation to the disposal of an overseas residence, the individual would be entitled to a credit for any tax paid against the individual's UK tax.

Law: TIOPA 2010, s. 9(2), 18(2)

2.4.3   Cases in which credit is not allowed

In order to prevent double relief or a windfall being created, if main or only residence relief is available fully or partially, a tax credit will not be allowable on foreign tax paid, and therefore lost, on the amount of main residence relief claimed.

Law: TIOPA 2010, s. 41

2.5   Disposals of UK residential property interests by non-residents – changes introduced by FA 2015

2.5.1   Historical background

These changes gained momentum after an announcement at *Autumn Statement* 2013, and a three-month consultation period in 2014. The Government published a draft *Finance Bill* 2015 for consultation on 10 December 2014 (see http://tinyurl.com/kszmkvb (a shortened link)) and Parliament enacted the changes (with few amendments) in FA 2015, s. 39 and Sch. 9. In a measure which represents a significant shift from the established principle that non-UK residents were not subject to CGT regardless of where the capital assets were held, the legislation contains (amongst others) a series of changes which affect the availability of main residence relief on disposals of UK residences by non-UK resident individuals, trusts and personal representatives. The changes came into effect in relation to disposals on or after 6 April 2015. The policy objective is described as "improving the fairness of the tax system by addressing the current imbalance between the treatment of UK residents and non-residents disposing of UK residential property".

The most interesting part about the FA 2015 amendments is that the two options envisaged by HMRC in order to address the perceived "unfairness" of tax treatment between UK-resident and non-UK resident taxpayers (as outlined in the consultation document published in 2014) have not been implemented. By way of background, these two options included the abolition of main residence relief elections and either:

(i)   establishing which of two or more properties should be treated as the individual's main residence based on a multi-factorial analysis of facts, taking into account factors such as the location of the individual's work and family; or

(ii)   introducing an entirely new objective test to be determined by HMRC and the tribunals, possibly based on days of presence at each of the properties.

Following consultation, it transpired that both of these options would introduce undesirable complexity in trying to ascertain which of two residences should be treated as a main residence and would unfairly affect some UK-resident individuals, possibly increasing tax bills. Both options were therefore rejected in favour of the proposals set out in FA 2015.

2.5.2   Summary of changes

In so far as relevant for this text, the changes in FA 2015 may be summarised as follows:

All references to "dwelling-house" include part of a dwelling-house. These rules also apply to UK resident individuals who own and dispose of a dwelling-house overseas and do not meet the day count test (see below).

Determination of main residence: non-UK resident CGT disposals

New TCGA 1992, s. 222A applies where an individual makes a disposal of a dwelling-house (or of an interest in a dwelling-house) which was occupied as a residence (or land occupied as its garden or grounds: see **4.2** below) and the disposal constitutes a "non-

26

resident CGT disposal" ("NRCGT"). In a nutshell, a NRCGT is defined by new TCGA 1992, s. 14B as a disposal of a UK residential property by:

> (i)   an individual, trustees of a settlement, personal representatives or any other person who is not UK resident for the relevant tax year or relevant time; or
>
> (ii)   an individual who is not UK resident where the gain on the disposal would accrue in the overseas part of a split year (under the residence rules in FA 2013).

Section 222A provides that where a person makes a disposal when non-resident, any determination as to which of two or more of his residences was his main residence for a period must be made in a specifically designed "advanced tax return". An election pursuant to this section cannot, however, vary a previous determination for a residence, the disposal of which has already occurred.

Periods of deemed absence for non-residents

A dwelling-house will be treated as not occupied as a residence for a tax year (this will be known as the "deeming rule") when it is located in a country in which the person is not resident for tax purposes and the person does not spend at least 90 midnights during the year there ("the day count test"). For the purposes of the day count test, any day spent in the dwelling-house by the individual's spouse or civil partner counts as a day spent by the individual in the dwelling-house. The number of midnights required will be reduced proportionally when the residence is owned for part of a tax year. Where the individual has more than one dwelling-house in the same country, the day count test will apply across all dwelling-houses and the number of midnights (which need not be consecutive) spent in each one of those houses will be aggregated. The individual may then nominate one to be subject to main residence relief (TCGA 1992, s. 222B and 222C).

Amount of relief

There will be no scope for main residence relief on both UK and non-UK residences during the same overlapping period (TCGA 1992, s. 223A).

The definition of "period of ownership" does not include ownership of an overseas dwelling-house prior to 6 April 2015 unless the non-UK resident individual elects otherwise and specifies a date as to when the dwelling was his only or main residence. This election must be made in the non-resident "advancement tax return" (TCGA 1992, s. 223A(1)-(3)).

When a non-UK resident individual disposes of a dwelling-house, the occupation of the dwelling or any absences are ignored in determining eligibility to main residence relief unless the individual makes an election. If an election is made, any absences from the date specified to 5 April 2015 are deducted from the amount of absence available for relief for periods after 5 April 2015 (TCGA 1992, s. 223A(4)-(6)).

All of the changes discussed above are reflected in corresponding amendments to TCGA 1992, s. 225 in respect of beneficiaries of a trust occupying a dwelling-house under the terms of the settlement (TCGA 1992, s. 225(1) and (2)).

Similarly, corresponding amendments were also made to TCGA 1992, s. 225A in respect of legatees of a deceased person occupying a dwelling-house under an entitlement as a legatee or an interest in possession (personal representatives: TCGA 1992, s. 225A(5) and (7)).

Compliance

Any CGT charge due will have to be paid within 30 days of the dwelling-house being conveyed (in line with stamp duty land tax), unless the person has a pre-existing self-assessment record with HMRC or has received a notice to file a tax return from HMRC for the relevant tax year. In those circumstances, the payment may be made on the due date for the tax year in which the disposal is made. It is important to note that the possible exemption from payment of the non-resident CGT does not apply to the filing of the NRCGT return. The duty to notify and file a return within 30 days of a relevant disposal still remains even if there is nil tax to pay or an incurred capital loss.

It is difficult to see how non-UK resident owners would be familiar with the new rules, and the duty to file NRCGT returns has resulted in a number of them incurring penalties, even though they have no other tax presence in the UK. Appeals against penalties have resulted in mixed outcomes in the FTT: for recent decisions, see *McGreevy*, *Saunders*, *Hesketh & Hesketh*, and *Welland*.

FA 2016, s. 91 removed the obligation to file an NRCGT return (or introduced the possibility of filing an elective NRCGT return) in two limited circumstances (new TMA 1970, s. 12ZBA). The first is when a disposal is treated as if neither a gain nor a loss accrues and the second is when a lease is granted at arm's length to an unconnected person for no premium. The effect of this provision is that in these two limited circumstances (more may be added from time to time by the Treasury) no penalty will be imposed for late NRCGT returns which are submitted but not required.

HMRC's Guidance *Capital Gains Tax for non-residents: UK residential property*, which (at the time of writing) was last updated on 7 August 2017, may be found online at www.gov.uk.

Law: TMA 1970, s. 12ZBA; TCGA 1992, s. 222A, 222B, 222C, 223A, 225(1), (2), 225A(5), (7); FA 2015, s. 39 and Sch. 9; FA 2016, s. 91

Cases: *McGreevy v HMRC* [2017] UKFTT 690 (TC); *Saunders v HMRC* [2017] UKFTT 765 (TC); *Welland v HMRC* [2017] UKFTT 870 (TC); *Hesketh & Hesketh v HMRC* [2017] UKFTT 871 (TC)

Guidance: https://www.gov.uk/guidance/capital-gains-tax-for-non-residents-uk-residential-property

3. Meaning of dwelling-house

3.1 No statutory definition in the Taxes Acts

3.1.1 No definition of "dwelling-house"

Under the general heading of "Private Residences" the opening words of s. 222 of TCGA 1992 read as follows:

222. Relief on disposal of private residence

(1) This section applies to a gain accruing to an individual so far as attributable to the disposal of, or of an interest in—

(a) a **dwelling-house** or **part of a dwelling-house** which is, or has at any time in his period of ownership been, his only or main residence, or .... .

Similarly to the term "residence" (and somewhat understandably), the term "dwelling-house" is not defined in the legislation and will therefore be subject to interpretation by HMRC and, if necessary, the courts depending on the facts of each case.

3.1.2 A new and simple definition of "dwelling" in TCGA 1992

The enactment of the new rules in FA 2016 on disposals of "residential property interests" ("RPI") (new TCGA 1992, Sch. 4ZZC inserted by FA 2016, s. 83 and Sch. 12, para. 5) marked the introduction of a brand new statutory definition of "dwelling" for the purposes of the new provisions. This is the only definition of "dwelling" now present in TCGA 1992 and it has two limbs depending on whether the disposal relates to an interest in the UK or outside the UK as follows:

UK RPI

In relation to a disposal of a UK residential property interest a building counts as a "dwelling" at any time when:

(a) it is used or suitable for use as a dwelling, or

(b) it is in the process of being constructed or adapted for such use.

30

Most helpful is the definition of what does *not* count as dwelling for these purposes. According to TCGA 1992, Sch. B1, para. 4(3)-(5) a building is not used (or suitable for use) as a dwelling if it is used as:

(a)   residential accommodation for school pupils;

(b)   residential accommodation for members of the armed forces;

(c)   a home or other institution providing residential accommodation for children;

(d)   a home or other institution providing residential accommodation with personal care for persons in need of personal care by reason of old age, disability, past or present dependence on alcohol or drugs or past or present mental disorder;

(e)   a hospital or hospice;

(f)   a prison or similar establishment

(g)   a hotel or inn or similar establishment; or

(h)   certain buildings occupied by students and managed or controlled by their educational establishment etc. as defined in the *Housing Act* 2004.

In the case of (a) to (f) above, a further condition is that the establishment is the sole or main residence of its residents.

Non-UK RPI

In relation to a disposal of a non-UK residential property interest, Sch. BA1 utilises a similar definition of dwelling (including paras (a) to (g) above) but excludes buildings occupied by students and managed or controlled by their educational establishment etc.

"Dwelling" narrower than "dwelling-house"

Of particular note is the fact that the definition of dwelling for the purpose of RPI disposals is limited to "buildings", so other places which could potentially be used as a dwelling (like boats or caravans) are excluded. This can be contrasted with the much wider definition of "dwelling-house" given in case law for main residence relief (see **3.4** below).

Law: FA 2016, s. 83 and Sch. 12, para. 5; TCGA 1992, Sch. B1, para. 4; Sch. BA1, para. 4

3.2 HMRC guidance

HMRC's *Capital Gains Manual* at CG 64230 does little more than warn readers that as there is no definition in TCGA 1992, s. 222, HMRC will be guided by the principles laid down in relevant case law[1]. CG 64230 does, however, accept that although in most cases, an entire building where an individual resides will be a "dwelling-house", there could be cases where the entity that makes up a "dwelling-house" could be made up of more than one building or even a smaller part of a building.

HMRC also recognise that there are instances where an individual lives in a location which does not fall within the ordinary definition of a dwelling-house but which may nevertheless be treated as that individual's residence. It is certainly correct to say that studying the decisions made in the past 60 years by the courts, the question of whether a place of abode represents a "dwelling-house" for the purposes of main residence relief is a matter of fact and degree to be determined by the tribunals or courts looking at all the circumstances in the round.

3.3 Assistance from other regimes

3.3.1 Town planning

In finding a definition for "dwelling-house", it would be helpful to explore whether there is such a definition in other statutes. A statutory regime which deals with the treatment of "dwelling-houses" for the purpose of development control and strategic planning is the *Town and Country Planning Act* 1990 and associated secondary legislation. In planning law a "dwelling-house" is treated as a concept of both design and use and although there is no comprehensive statutory definition, McCullough J observed in *Gravesham BC*:

> "In using a simple word in common usage and leaving it undefined, Parliament realistically expected that, in the overwhelming majority of cases, there would be no difficulty at all in deciding whether a particular building was or was not a dwelling-house. The use in a statute of almost any word in

---

[1] It should be noted, however, that the topic was revised in October 2010 with regards to capital allowances in CA 11520.

common usage may give rise to difficulties of interpretation in a very small number of cases, but the problems are both fewer and less troublesome than those that are apt to result when the statute defines the word."

The definition provided in the *Town & Country (General Permitted Development) Order* 1995 is an exclusive one (art. 1(2)) in that it states what a "dwelling-house" is not: it does not include a building containing one or more flats, or a flat contained within such a building. A flat is defined at art. 1(2) as:

"A separate and self-contained set of premises constructed for use for the purpose of a dwelling and forming part of a building from some other part of which it is divided horizontally."

Thus, if a dwelling does not occupy all floors of the building, it will constitute a "flat" rather than a dwelling-house, but will still be treated as a "dwelling". In the *Gravesham BC* case, McCullough J identified further that whatever the physical division, in order to be treated as a dwelling, the building must still be a house for dwelling in.

Case: *Gravesham BC v. Secretary of State for the Environment* (1984) 47 P & CR 142

3.3.2   Housing

Legislation on housing-related matters is of no further help: the interpretation sections of the *Housing Act* 1985, s. 112 and the *Housing Act* 1988, s. 45(1) explain that a dwelling-house "may be a house or part of a house" but offer no further definition.

3.3.3   Housing – Supreme Court authority – November 2014

In the case of *R (on the applications of ZH and CN)* a Supreme Court judgment released on 12 November 2014 deals directly with the question of what the word "dwelling" means in the context of a "licence to occupy premises as a dwelling" (for the purposes of the *Housing Act* 1996 and the *Protection from Eviction Act* 1977). The Court held (by majority) that:

"26. The word "dwelling" is not a technical word with a precise scientific meaning. Nor does it have a fixed meaning.

Words such as "live at", "reside" and "dwell" are ordinary words of the English language, as is "home".

More recently, in *Uratemp Ventures Ltd v Collins* [2002] 1 AC 301 the speeches in the House of Lords showed that the word "dwelling" had different shades of meaning. Lord Bingham of Cornhill (at para 10) said that a "dwelling-house" was "the place where someone dwells, lives or resides". Lord Steyn (at para 15) suggested that the court should not put restrictive glosses on the word which conveyed the idea of a place where someone lived. Lord Millett said (at para 30):

> "The words 'dwell' and 'dwelling' are not terms of art with a specialised legal meaning. They are ordinary English words, even if they are perhaps no longer in common use. They mean the same as 'inhabit' and 'habitation' or more precisely 'abide' and 'abode', and refer to the place where one lives and makes one's home. They suggest a greater degree of settled occupation than 'reside' and 'residence', connoting the place where the occupier habitually sleeps and usually eats, ..."

In my view there is no strict hierarchy in terms of settled occupation between the words "live at", "reside" and "dwell" and much may depend on the context in which the words are used. But there are nuances and as a general rule I agree with Lord Millett that "dwelling" suggests a greater degree of settled occupation than "residence"."

Later on in the judgment, after an analysis of the relevant case law dealing with the housing legislation, Lord Hodge (delivering the decision of the majority) concluded:

> "45. Pulling together the threads of the case law, in my view the following can be stated:
>
> (i)   the words "live at", "reside" and "dwell" are ordinary words of the English language and do not have technical meanings,
>
> (ii)   those words must be interpreted in the statutes in which they appear having regard to the purpose of those enactments,

(iii) as a matter of nuance, "dwelling" as a general rule suggests a more settled occupation than "residence" and can be equated with one's home, although "residence" itself can in certain contexts (such as the two-home cases) require such an equation, and

(iv) [specific to the Housing Acts and not reproduced here]."

With the assistance of this recent guidance from the Supreme Court on the definition of "dwelling", it would be fair to say that "dwelling-house" will be interpreted according to the purpose of TCGA 1992 and main residence relief. In other words, the legislation aims to provide relief from CGT on the disposal of an individual's "home" as would be interpreted by the reasonable man on the street.

Law: *Housing Act* 1985, s. 112; *Housing Act* 1988, s. 45(1); TCGA 1992, s. 222(1)(a); *Town & Country (General Permitted Development) Order* 1995, Art. 1(2)
Cases: *Gravesham BC v. Secretary of State for the Environment* (1984) 47 P & CR 142; *R (on the application of ZH and CN) v London Borough of Newham and London Borough of Lewisham* [2014] UKSC 62
Guidance: CG 64230

3.4   What could also be considered a "dwelling-house"?

3.4.1   *Accommodation considered "unconventional"*

As there is no set definition of "dwelling-house" in TCGA 1992 (or anywhere else), there is scope for flexibility when considering a place which has been used as a dwelling but which does not fall within what would ordinarily be considered a "house" because it is not built out of brick and mortar or because an individual takes residence in a building constructed for other uses/purposes and occupies some of the rooms as a "dwelling-house". For instance a factory building, a purpose built hotel or hostel, a caravan or a houseboat.

3.4.2   *HMRC guidance – relationship with the exemption for chattels*

HMRC's *Capital Gains Manual* at CG 64325 explains that if a caravan is a tangible moveable asset (chattel) and a wasting asset and no capital allowances were or could be claimed on its cost, then no chargeable gain can arise on a subsequent disposal. However, if the caravan is so fixed to the land on which it is placed (and not capable of being easily moved) as to become a fixture on the land, it will cease to be treated as a chattel and any disposal would be subject to CGT. If such a caravan has been used as a home for all intents and purposes, it may be regarded as a "dwelling-house" and main residence relief may be available.

Planning tip

The wasting assets exemption in TCGA 1992, s. 45(1) dictates that no chargeable gain will accrue on the disposal of a chattel which has a predictable useful life of 50 years or less (wasting asset). If this exemption is likely to apply to a caravan, houseboat or other structure used as a residence owned by an individual, the most favourable treatment would be to invoke this exemption before any claim for main residence relief (which may be restricted by partial business use or periods of absence). Since this exemption prevents a chargeable gain from accruing, rather than rendering a gain which would otherwise be a chargeable gain as not chargeable, there is a strong motivation for insisting that the disposal of the asset is treated under the CGT chattel exemption.

The principle of a claim for main residence relief in relation to a caravan (or other unconventional accommodation used as a residence) emerged from two (slightly contradictory) cases decided in 1976 and 1986 in the High Court, Chancery Division.

3.4.3   Makins v Elson – a jacked up and fully-serviced caravan

In this case, the taxpayer purchased land with outline planning permission for building a house in July 1970. He moved onto the land in August 1970 with his family and lived there in two caravans. He started building operations in September 1970 but very little had actually been constructed by the time he sold the land and one of the caravans in May 1973. Although the caravan in question had wheels, during the time of occupation it had been jacked up and rested on some sort of supports. The caravan had the benefit of a telephone, electricity and water supply. The High Court decided that although "the very particular facts of this case will [not] in fact apply to a great many others", the fact that this caravan had electricity, water and a telephone and its wheels were not on the ground meant that the caravan was for the relevant period a dwelling-house and the taxpayer's only or main residence within the meaning of FA 1965, s. 29(1).

Case: *Makins v Elson* [1977] 1 WLR 22, (1976) 51 TC 437

3.4.4   Moore v Thompson – a "builder's" caravan

In direct contrast, in *Moore v Thompson,* the taxpayer purchased an old farmhouse which was uninhabitable and in need of renovation and updating work. The taxpayer brought a caravan onto the site and kept it in the courtyard during the building works. The caravan had no electricity, water or any other services connected to it but the taxpayer stayed in it from time to time. After the renovation and building work had ended, the taxpayer disposed of the farmhouse and grounds and claimed main residence relief exemption for the entire period of ownership despite not being able to live in the main house for many months.

The General Commissioners found that the taxpayer's stays in the caravan were "sporadic and occasional" and did not have the degree of permanence or continuity to make it a residence. Millet J endorsed this finding and held that:

> "It is clear that the Commissioners were alive to the fact that even occasional and short residence in a place can make it a residence; but the question is one of fact and degree for the Commissioners."

Case: *Moore v Thompson (HMIT)* [1986] STC 170, 60 TC 15

3.4.5   A houseboat

According to HMRC's guidance at CG 64328, the same principles which apply to caravans will also apply to a boat which is used as a dwelling in terms of identifying it as a "dwelling-house" for the purpose of the legislation.

As a general rule, HMRC require the houseboat to be permanently located on the site (and without the possibility of moving) and connected to all mains services for at least six months in order to be treated as automatically falling within the definition of "dwelling-house". In other circumstances, each individual case will be considered on its own specific facts.

If a yacht, barge or other boat is used as the residence of its owner, and its useful life is longer than 50 years, a chargeable gain may also arise on its disposal. Main residence relief may be available too but only if this type of vessel has been occupied as a home (and in accordance with the principles in *Makins*).

Case: *Makins v Elson* [1977] 1 WLR 22, (1976) 51 TC 437

3.4.6 Replacement house – impact of demolition and rebuilding

There is no indication on the strict literal reading of s. 222(1) of whether or not main residence relief is available in circumstances where a dwelling-house used as a main or only residence is demolished (deliberately or due to accidental damage or to an "act of God") and a brand new house is immediately constructed to replace it *in situ*. It is not immediately clear whether "dwelling-house" refers to the building structure itself which includes as an ancillary matter the land on which it is sited or to the land, which includes as an ancillary matter the building sited on it.

This exact point was analysed and decided by the First-tier Tribunal in the relatively recent case of *Gibson*. In that case, the owner of the original dwelling-house had enquired about renovating and extending the existing accommodation and had been advised by his architects that it would be cheaper in the long term to demolish the existing house in its entirety and to build a new one from scratch. For these purposes, HMRC accepted that the original house was the taxpayer's only or main residence and the Tribunal proceeded to consider the case on the basis that the original dwelling-house had been the taxpayer's only or main residence and that his intention to sell it was formed after some time of it being occupied as a residence.

The main question for the Tribunal to decide was whether the original house and the brand new house were the same "dwelling-house" within the meaning of s. 222(1) TCGA 1992. In weighing up all factors in favour of and against a conclusion that the two houses were the same dwelling-house, the Tribunal considered:

- As a matter of ordinary language, it could be said that the original house had ceased to exist and that an entirely new house had been erected in its place. As a result they could not be considered as one and the same dwelling-house.

- Having said that, the Tribunal believed the reason provided by the taxpayer for demolishing the existing house and building a new one and it was arguable that there is no reason for ascribing different tax consequences to remodelling and renovating the existing house and rebuilding just because they were different means to the same end.

- There could be difficulties in distinguishing between the two cases in practice. For instance, is a house remodelled and renovated or entirely rebuilt if its foundations are kept or if the same materials are used in the reconstruction?

- It may be unjust to apply a different tax treatment in cases where the demolition of the original house is outside the taxpayer's control (e.g. destruction by fire).

- It is not a requirement of the legislation to utilise the proceeds of a disposal of a residence to fund the purchase of a new home and so it was an irrelevant consideration in the circumstances.

It had been argued that the intention of Parliament could not have been to use the words in their ordinary meaning. By majority decision, the Tribunal (Judge Staker and Member De Albuquerque) decided that the considerations highlighted above were not enough to justify that conclusion. In summary: "if one house is completely demolished and a new house erected in the same location, then the new house is not the same 'dwelling-house' as the one that previously stood on that site".

In the author's opinion (and despite the Tribunal not taking it into account), this decision is entirely consistent with the decision of the Court of Appeal in *Ellis & Sons v Sisman* which (although not a tax case and not on all fours with the legislature) came to the same conclusion.

In *Sisman* a house within the *Rent Restriction Acts* (as applicable in 1947) was so extensively damaged in World War II that it had to be

39

demolished by the local authority. The claimant was the protected tenant of the house. After the war the landlords proceeded to construct on the site another house similar in all respects to the one demolished. The tenant claimed that he had the same rights of occupation over the new house as he did over the original house and argued that as there was land let with the original dwelling-house, it became for the purpose of the Acts part of the dwelling-house, and that the land has always remained, even if the dwelling-house had ceased to exist, so that the plot of land had remained at all times part of the dwelling-house. Tucker LJ held[2] that he found it:

> "difficult to see how something which has to be treated as part of something else can still be regarded as part of that something else when that something else has ceased to exist".

Cases: *Ellis & Sons Amalgamated Properties, Limited v Sisman* [1948] 1 KB 653; *Gibson v HMRC* [2013] UKFTT 636 (TC)

3.4.7 Destroyed dwelling-houses

Taking into account the courts' interpretation of the term "dwelling-house" and the actual wording in s. 222(1)(a) "disposal of…a dwelling-house", it naturally follows that if a house is completely destroyed or demolished, there will be no "dwelling-house" in existence and therefore no main residence relief.

It should be noted that in this circumstance, it is open to the owner of the land to make a negligible value claim under TCGA 1992, s. 24(3) in "the occasion of the entire loss, destruction, dissipation or extinction of an asset". In that case, the owner of the land and of the destroyed building, will be deemed to make a disposal of the building and "shall be treated as if he had also sold, and immediately reacquired, the site of the building or structure (including in the site any land occupied for purposes ancillary to the use of the building or structure) for a consideration equal to its market value at that time".

3.4.8 Abandoned or derelict dwelling-houses

There is no specific provision or case that deals with this exact point but in the author's view, if a dwelling-house has been occupied as an individual's main or only residence during a part of the ownership,

---

[2] At p 666.

the fact that the house may have been abandoned or became derelict (which is in itself a question of fact and degree for a Tribunal to decide) does not invalidate a claim for main residence relief. As such a house fell within the definition of a dwelling-house occupied as a residence at some point in the period of ownership, in the absence of a change of use, the house is unlikely to lose its status as "dwelling-house" for the purpose of calculating the appropriate amount of relief due (adjustment).

This view seems to be supported by the decision of the High Court in the property case of *In Re 1-4, White Row Cottages* where the Court decided that:

> " 'dwelling-house,' properly construed as a matter of ordinary language in the context of [the *Common Land (Rectification of Registers) Act* 1989], did not necessarily connote actual residence but could include an unoccupied or derelict house or one which had been condemned as unfit for human habitation; that, similarly, the words "used and enjoyed" in the context of subsection (3) did not necessarily contemplate actual use and enjoyment of a garden, garage or outbuildings ancillary to a dwelling-house; and that, therefore, the requirements specified in section 1(2) were satisfied in respect of the cottages".

Law: TCGA 1992, s. 24(1), (3), 45(1), 222(1)(a)
Case: *In Re 1-4, White Row Cottages, Bewerley,* [1991] 3 WLR 229
Guidance: CG 64328

3.5 Part of a dwelling-house – the entity of the dwelling-house

3.5.1 *Appurtenant to and within the curtilage of a dwelling-house*

In a similar vein, main residence relief does not apply exclusively to a "dwelling-house" (or structure used as such); if an individual disposes of *part* of a dwelling-house which has been used as his main residence then the relief will, in theory, be available.

"In theory", because there is a requirement that a building cannot form part of a "dwelling-house" which includes a main house unless the building (or structure) is within the curtilage of the main house and appurtenant to the main house.

3.5.2   Defining "curtilage" – general principles

Despite the use of this term being fairly widespread in legislation and in decisions and Court judgments, there is no statutory definition of the word. Analogous to the (lack of) definition of residence and dwelling-house, as the word is not specifically defined in statute, courts will have to apply it using its everyday, ordinary meaning. Help may be obtained from the following.

3.5.3   "Curtilage" – dictionary definitions

Oxford Dictionary

> "A small court, yard, garth, or piece of ground attached to a dwelling-house, and forming one enclosure with it, or so regarded by the law; the area to and containing a dwelling-house and its outbuildings."

New Oxford Dictionary of English (Clarendon, Oxford, 1988)

> "An area of land attached to a house and forming one enclosure with it."

Stroud's Judicial Dictionary

> "A garden, yard, field, or peece of voide ground. Laying neare and belonging to the messuage (Termes de la Ley)."

The common denominators in these dictionary definitions are a small size, close proximity and a degree of physical attachment to the main dwelling-house. Bearing this in mind, it will be helpful to see how these definitions have been applied to real-life settings.

3.5.4   "Curtilage" – cases decided under various statutory regimes

"Curtilage" is a concept widely used in other areas of law and in other statutory contexts. Decisions and judgments which explain the meaning of the term whilst analysing other statutory regimes provide insightful interpretations and the basis for factual comparison.

3.5.5   *Housing*

The leading housing case on the meaning of curtilage is *Dyer v Dorset County Council*, a Court of Appeal case that arose under the *Housing Act* 1980, in which the Court held that in the absence of any definition, "curtilage" bore its restricted and established meaning connoting a small area forming part and parcel of the house or building which it contained or to which it was attached. It was further held that it was ultimately a matter of fact and degree in each case. In that case, the Court found it impossible to accept that the house – occupied by the applicant and within but on the edge of the grounds of a college and separated by a significant amount of green land – was within the curtilage of the main college building. Nourse LJ endorsed as adequate the definition contained in the Oxford English Dictionary as explained above.

Similarly, in the case of *Sinclair-Lockhart's Trustees*, the Court of Session held that the word "curtilage" could be described as follows:

> "The ground which is used for the comfortable enjoyment of a house or other building may be regarded in law as being within the curtilage of that house or building and thereby as an integral part of the same although it has not been marked off or enclosed in any way. It is enough that it serves the purpose of the house or building in some necessary or reasonably useful way."

In the author's view, this definition is unsatisfactory and a little inaccurate as it could potentially include a neighbouring garden or drive which serve a house in a "reasonably useful way" by providing an attractive view or an alternative access but which is clearly not part of the main dwelling-house. It should also be noted that in the nineteenth century case of *Caledonian Railway Co*, the House of Lords held that an access way leading to a yard could, in appropriate circumstances, be part of the curtilage of the building adjoining the yard. It naturally followed that the access way in question could not be severed from the rest of the property being compulsorily acquired without having a material detriment on the rest of the land.

Cases: *Caledonian Railway Co v Turcan* [1898] AC 256; *Dyer v Dorset County Council* [1989] 1 QB 346; *Sinclair-Lockhart's Trustees and Collins v Secretary of State* [1989] EGCS 15

3.5.6   Town planning and ecclesiastical law

The following conclusions may be also be derived from looking at the cases in this area.

No size limit

First, the curtilage of a building need not always be a small area: *Skerritts*. This fairly recent case concerned the Grade II listed Grimsdyke Hotel, in Harrow. The owners of the hotel had installed double glazing in a stable block situated some 200 metres from the hotel. As no listed building consent had been obtained for the operation, the planning authority began enforcement proceedings, on the basis that the stable block lay within the curtilage of the hotel and therefore consent should have been obtained. The company maintained that, based upon the decision in *Dyer*, no listed building consent was needed since the curtilage of a building had to be inherently small. The Court of appeal held that:

> "Whilst the decision in Dyer was plainly correct ... [the] court went further than it was necessary in expressing the view that the curtilage of a building must always be small, or that the notion of smallness is inherent in the expression[3]."

That is to say – and contrary to the ordinary dictionary meaning – the starting position in identifying a curtilage should not necessarily be that it is limited in size.

Historical evidence

Secondly, the extent of a dwelling-house's curtilage and what it encompasses is essentially a question of fact and degree but a decision-maker may be assisted by historical data.

---

[3] As per Robert Walker LJ at p 519. It was decided that the Inspector and Secretary of State had not erred in law in not making a particular reference to smallness and concluding that building consent was indeed needed because in the context of substantial listed buildings the curtilage was likely to extend to what were or had been, in terms of ownership and function, ancillary buildings.

The Court in *Skerritts* did not venture into giving any further guidance on the approach to be taken when determining what exactly is within the curtilage of a building and it limited itself to reiterating the position established in *Dyer* that it is always a question of fact and degree. This case also reinforced the decisions previously reached by the courts in *James* and *McAlpine*.

In *James*, the court upheld an Inspector's finding that a tennis court built at the end of a field some 100 metres away from the dwelling-house was not within its curtilage. It was found that the field was separate and distinct from the cultivated garden attached to the house and that the house and the tennis court did not have the appearance of being within this same enclosure. The Court maintained that it was quintessentially a matter of fact.

In *McAlpine*, the court upheld an enforcement notice requiring the removal of a swimming pool which had been constructed without planning permission in the grounds of a substantial listed building. There was a garden at the rear of the main house and beyond that an extensive open-grassed area which had been used for generations for recreation as part of the garden. The Court held that whether the pool was in the curtilage of the listed house was essentially a matter of fact and degree for the Inspector to determine. The learned judge also held that it was open to inspectors, in appropriate cases, to consider historical evidence where it assisted the determination of the current curtilage boundary.

Ownership and legal title

Thirdly, the curtilage of a building or dwelling should not necessarily be equated to land in the same ownership: *Lowe*. Notwithstanding this established principle, in ecclesiastical law, for unconsecrated land to be in the 'curtilage' of a church within section 7 of the *Faculty Jurisdiction Measure* 1964 (No. 5), both must be occupied together and belong together in a physical sense, their titles not being such as to conflict with their belonging together (*Re St. George's Church, Oakdale*).

Finally, the curtilage should serve the purpose of the main dwelling or building in some necessary or useful manner (*Sinclair-Lockhart's Trustees*).

Cases: *Re St. George's Church, Oakdale* [1976] Fam 210; *Sinclair-Lockhart's Trustees and Collins v Secretary of State* [1989] EGCS 15; *Dyer v Dorset County Council* [1989] 1 QB 346; *James v Secretary of State* [1991] 1 PLR 58; *McAlpine v Secretary of State* [1995] 1 PLR 16; *Skerritts of Nottingham Ltd v Secretary of State for the Environment, Transport and the Regions* [2000] 3 WLR 511; *Lowe v First Secretary of State* [2003] 1 PLR 81

3.5.7   "Curtilage" – capital gains tax – HMRC's view

In their guidance at CG 64245, HMRC have gone for the simplest approach and have adopted the definition in the *Oxford Dictionary* thus:

> "The word curtilage is defined by the Shorter Oxford Dictionary as, "a small court, yard, or piece of ground, attached to a dwelling-house and forming one enclosure with it". This definition of the word was quoted in *Methuen-Campbell v Walters* (see below). When setting down the 'curtilage test' emphasis was placed on the smallness of the area. So buildings standing around a courtyard together with the main house will be within the curtilage of the main house. Where such buildings have a residential use, they will be included within the entity making up the dwelling-house. It is important to remember that in order to be part of the entity of the dwelling-house, the building must have a residential purpose regardless to its closeness to the dwelling-house.
>
> In the *Leasehold Reform Act* case of *Methuen-Campbell v Walters*, which is quoted with approval by the Court of Appeal in *Lewis v Rook*, it was noted that there may be occasions where more dispersed buildings will fall within a single curtilage if their relationship with each other is such that they constitute an integral whole."

3.5.8   "Curtilage" – according to case law

Before the early 1990s, there was no guidance or set rule on the factors to be taken into account when identifying the entity of a dwelling-house. There were a few conflicting decisions by the High Court and it seemed that the conclusion as to whether a building

46

was part of a dwelling-house depended on the views of the particular judge who happened to apply the principles (as he saw them) to the facts in hand.

3.5.9 *Batey v Wakefield – independent caretaker's cottage may still be part of a dwelling-house*

The first important case to deal with the issue of curtilage was *Batey v Wakefield*. In that case, the taxpayer constructed a four-bedroom house within 1.1 acres of land. The taxpayer's employment required him to live in London in a flat which he first rented but then purchased and as a result the house was left unattended whilst he was working in London. As a consequence of the house (and others in the neighbouring area) being burgled, the taxpayer decided to employ a caretaker/gardener and housekeeper (husband and wife) to look after the house and proceeded to build a bungalow to accommodate them. The bungalow had its own access to a separate road and was separated from the main house by an already established yew hedge and by the width of a tennis court. A number of years later the flat was sold, the main house was occupied permanently and there was no longer a need for a full-time caretaker. The bungalow was sold with 0.15 acres of land and the taxpayer contended that the gain on the disposal was exempt pursuant to s. 29(2) of FA 1965 because it was part of the dwelling-house which had been occupied as his main residence.

The Revenue contended that the bungalow did not form part of the taxpayer's dwelling-house because the properties were not only physically separated by a hedge but were also rated individually. Furthermore, there was a separate access to it and the bungalow had been disposed of separately. It was argued that the separate disposal of the bungalow was an indication that such land was not required for the reasonable enjoyment of the main house as a residence. The general view adopted by the Revenue then was that a physically separated ancillary dwelling-house could not be part of another dwelling.

The Commissioners decided that a dwelling-house could comprise more than one building on the same site not being adjoining buildings. The bungalow was occupied in conjunction with the main house, having been built specifically for staff purposes and to increase the taxpayer's reasonable enjoyment of the house. The

Chancery Division agreed with this analysis, adding that the taxpayer's house and residence consisted of all those buildings which were part and parcel of the whole, each part being appurtenant to and occupied for the purposes of the residence (e.g. garages, potting sheds, greenhouses, stables and summer houses):

> "What [is] the residence of the taxpayer? For that purpose, you have to identify the dwelling-house which is his residence. That dwelling-house may or may not be comprised in one physical building; it may comprise a number of different buildings. His dwelling-house and residence consists of all those buildings which are part and parcel of the whole, each part being appurtenant to and occupied for the purpose of the residence." (per Browne-Wilkinson J at 577).

Not being satisfied by these two decisions, the Revenue appealed to the Court of Appeal. The appellate Court also disagreed with the Revenue's interpretation of the law and Fox LJ said at p. 560:

> "Browne-Wilkinson J. in his judgment said this: 'On the commissioners' findings, the lodge was built and occupied to provide services and caretaking facilities for the benefit of the main house. The lodge was occupied by the taxpayer through his employee, who was employed for the purpose of promoting the taxpayer's reasonable enjoyment of his own residence. In those circumstances, bearing in mind the fact that the buildings are very closely adjacent, it seems to me proper to find that the lodge was part of the residence of the taxpayer...' I agree with that."

The Court of Appeal gave clear guidance as to the factors to be taken into account in determining the entity of a dwelling-house:

(i)   A residence or dwelling-house can include several buildings which are used as dwellings but still distinctly separated from each other. The Court envisaged a situation where, although inconvenient, an individual could have a dwelling-house containing his living space and another ancillary dwelling containing his bedrooms and washing facilities. The fact that they would be separate would not prevent them from being a single dwelling-house.

(ii)   A taxpayer's dwelling-house could include another person's dwelling-house if the use of the latter was for the purpose of serving the former as a residence (staff accommodation).

(iii) It was a question of fact and degree for the Commissioners to determine.

Cases: *Batey (HMIT) v Wakefield* [1980] STC 572, [1980] TR 237, HC; *Batey (HMIT) v Wakefield* [1981] STC 521, [1981] 55 TC 550, CoA

3.5.10   *Green v IRC – unused parts may still be part of a dwelling-house*

The reasoning of the Court of Appeal in *Batey* was followed in *Green v CIR* by the First Division of the Inner House of the Court of Session in Scotland to dismiss a taxpayer's appeal against the decision of the Commissioners that the two wings of a mansion house, although closely adjacent and occupied for the purposes of the main house, were not to be taken as part of it for CGT purposes.

The facts of the case were presented in a rather convoluted detail in the decision of the Inner House but briefly Mr Green, an auctioneer by trade, purchased a large property comprising of 15 acres of land, a mansion house (with 33 rooms), two pavilions or wings (East and West) and two detached gazebos. Mr Green (along with his family and friends) had carried out substantial works of improvement and redecoration before finally moving into the mansion house. The east wing was occupied by a gardener cum handyman and his family for most of the period of ownership and the mansion house and two wings were on the valuation roll as separate rateable units of occupation. Each wing had its own separate entrance although there were connecting passages with the main house at basement level. Only certain rooms of the mansion house were in "apparent" use although every room was used for residential use/ occupation. The entire property was sold to the local Council when Mr Green fell into financial difficulties and he was assessed to CGT on the whole gain on disposal. The Revenue argued that:

- the gain on the mansion house should be apportioned into residential and business use (two auctions had been carried out within the house);

49

- to apportion the gain[4] on the mansion house on the basis that only part of the house was occupied as the taxpayer's main residence (some rooms were not in use "and the house was bigger than the household required" – a "startling proposition" as far as the Court was concerned);
- the East and West wings did not form part as a single entity of the taxpayer's main dwelling-house.

The Court decided (reluctantly) that the question to be asked was not what the court would have decided on the facts but whether the General Commissioners were entitled based on those facts to reach that particular decision on the matter. They decided that – in agreement with the decision in *Batey*:

> "A residence or a dwelling-house for the purposes of section 29 [FA 1965] can consist of more than one building, and that where there are buildings, such as the mansion house and the wings here, within a common curtilage and single ownership, and capable of being regarded as separate to some extent, what has to be determined is the identity of the taxpayer's residence."

It was a matter of degree whether a building does or does not form part of the residence in question and it was open to the Commissioners to conclude that the wings did not form part of the mansion dwelling-house.

Contrary to their "startling" arguments in this case and clearly following very unsubtle guidance from the Court, HMRC now accept in their manual at CG 64750:

> "Private residence relief should not be restricted because a person resides in a dwelling-house which is too big for them to use fully. Similarly, relief should not be restricted because some part of the dwelling-house has been left unused for a time. An attempt to restrict relief for that reason was rejected by the Court of Session in *Green v CIR* (56 TC 10).

---

[4] According to what is now TCGA 1992, s. 222(10).

However disuse may be a factor in deciding whether an ancillary building can be regarded as part of the entity which makes up the dwelling-house in which an individual has their only or main residence."

Case: *Green v CIR* [1982] BTC 378
Guidance: CG 64750

3.5.11   1980s – Proximity and reasonable enjoyment tests

In *Markey v Sanders*, a case heard seven years after *Batey*, the Chancery Division (Walton J) affirmed the dicta by Browne-Wilkinson J and summarised the conditions that have to be satisfied before a taxpayer can claim that a building which is not itself occupied as his main residence also constitutes his dwelling-house. The ancillary building must be:

- occupied in order to increase the owner's enjoyment of the main house; and
- "very closely adjacent" to the main building (this being a necessary but not sufficient condition).

The taxpayer in the case owned and occupied a small country estate of some 12¾ acres of land, a main house and a number of outbuildings. In 1965 she had constructed a detached three-bedroom staff bungalow located 130 metres away which was occupied rent-free by her gardener and housekeeper. The bungalow was separate from the main house and was screened by trees; it also had its own garden. The Revenue refused a claim for main residence relief on the disposal of the whole property including the staff bungalow on the basis that the bungalow was not sufficiently proximate to the house to form a single dwelling-house for the purposes of the relief. The General Commissioners disagreed with the Revenue and allowed the taxpayer's appeal.

Walton J reformulated the relevant test as follows:

"Now I myself would prefer to ask: looking at the group of buildings in question as a whole, is it fairly possible to regard them as a single dwelling-house used as the taxpayer's main residence?"

In the learned judge's view the "closely adjacent" test was imprecise and did not necessarily take into account the scale of the buildings in question. Bearing in mind the guidance laid down by the Court of Appeal in *Batey*, Walton J decided that since the country house was small, the bungalow had as many bedrooms as the main house and the bungalow was deliberately sited away from the house and physically separated by a paddock and screened by a ha-ha and a belt of trees, it was "utterly impossible to think that anybody, under any circumstances, could regard them as all one residence".

Thus, the final conclusion was that the Commissioners had come to a finding of fact that no other tribunal properly directed as to the law would have come to in the circumstances, and the Revenue's appeal was therefore allowed.

Case: *Markey v Sanders* [1987] STC 256; 60 TC 245

3.5.12 "Entity" – a single test

In *Williams v Merrylees* the court analysed the tests used by the Chancery Division in *Markey* and disagreed with the approach taken. In that case the taxpayer also owned a country estate set in four acres of land. The estate consisted of a four-bedroom house, stables and outbuildings and a four-bedroom lodge 200 metres away from the main house that was contemporaneously built. The lodge was occupied by the taxpayer's gardener, caretaker and housekeeper and had its separate entrance from the highway and was distinctly rated. The taxpayer sold the main house and most of the land in 1976 and the lodge and remaining land in 1979. He was assessed to CGT on the 1979 disposal and on appeal to the General Commissioners, they held that the lodge had been part of the taxpayer's only or main residence and was within the curtilage of the property and appurtenant to the main house at the relevant times.

Vinelott J expressed "very considerable doubt" that one could distil from the decision in *Batey* two distinct conditions that had to be fulfilled before an ancillary building could be considered part of a dwelling-house. The learned judge considered that both the High Court and the Court of Appeal had meant to lay down one single test and that no factor should be isolated in coming to that decision. The Court held that what the Commissioners had to look for was:

"an entity which can be sensibly described as being a dwelling-house although split up into different buildings performing different functions".

On the facts of the case, the Court – although stating that if making findings of fact, it may have decided otherwise – could identify no unreasonable finding by the General Commissioners and dismissed the appeal.

Cases: *Markey v Sanders* [1987] STC 256; 60 TC 245; *Williams v Merrylees* [1987] STC 445, 60 TC 297

3.5.13 *Within the curtilage of and appurtenant to the dwelling-house*

As the facts of the two cases discussed above were similar and the conclusions reached by two differently-constituted courts contradictory, it was very difficult to reconcile the decisions and to predict or advise on whether an ancillary building could be classified as part of a dwelling-house. The Court of Appeal was made aware of the ambiguity created by *Markey* and *Williams* in early 1992 in an appeal by Lady Beryl Rook against an assessment to CGT in relation to the sale of a cottage within the grounds of her country estate in Kent.

The estate was set in 10 acres of land and contained two semi-detached cottages situated about 175 metres away from the main house. One of the cottages had its own frontage to the highway, was individually rated and had been occupied at all relevant times by the taxpayer's gardener. The house and the cottage had not been separated or screened from each other and in fact, the elderly taxpayer could see the lights in the cottage and ring a ship's bell or flash a light for assistance in times of need. Once the gardener left in 1978, the taxpayer sold it and claimed main residence relief on the gain realised.

The Revenue accepted that the occupation by the gardener was occupation by the taxpayer but refused the claim on the ground that the cottage did not form part of the dwelling-house. The Commissioners found that on the evidence presented to them, the first cottage formed part of the entity which comprised the main house. On appeal from that decision, the High Court held that the entity constituting the taxpayer's residence included the first cottage because the taxpayer's way of living embraced use not only of the main house itself with its gardens but also of the cottage of the gardener who cared for those gardens. He further added that the distance between the house and the cottage was not determinative but that the set-up described above was.

The Court of Appeal did:

> "not find the current state of the authorities very satisfactory, and it is not surprising that different sets of General Commissioners have reached conclusions which are not always easy to understand".

The Court discussed the findings in *Batey*, *Markey* and *Williams* and held that simply identifying the taxpayer's "residence" would be a circular and confusing approach because in cases where the dwelling-house forms part of a small estate, it would be easy to consider the estate as the residence and therefore to conclude that all the buildings within the estate are part of the taxpayer's residence. It was consequently decided that the right formula to be used was a combination of what the Appeal Court had held in *Batey* and what was decided in *Dyer*. Their Lordships expressed approval for the notion of smallness of the area to be comprised in the curtilage (*Dyer*) and the "very closely" adjacent test (*Batey*) when determining what is within the curtilage of a dwelling-house or building. Balcombe LJ, delivering the judgment of the Court, confirmed that the right test to be applied should have been:

> "Was the cottage within the curtilage of, and appurtenant to, [the main house], so as to be a part of the entity which, together with Newlands, constituted the dwelling-house occupied by the taxpayer as her residence?"[5]

The learned judge went on to conclude that by reason of the distance, degree of separation and size of the estate, and applying the correct test, the Commissioners and the Court below should have found that the cottage was not within the curtilage of, and appurtenant to, the main house, and thus was not part of the entity which constituted the taxpayer's dwelling-house.

---

[5] At p 109.

Ritchie & Ritchie v HMRC – a shed may be part of and appurtenant to the dwelling-house

Mr and Mrs Ritchie bought land just outside of Moneymore, Co. Londonderry in 1987. The land purchased was part of the old dismantled train station and railway line. There were two buildings present on the land, a large shed which had stood on the old western platform and a small "potting" shed. The FTT found that the total area of the site was 0.669 hectares (the total area had been subject to dispute). The Ritchie family used the large shed to store children's toys, the family car, various tools, firewood and vegetables and also the ploughs which the husband used in ploughing competitions. The Ritchie family rented another house in the close proximity of the land. They obtained planning permission in 1991, built a substantial three storey house together with front and back gardens and moved in 1995. In June 2006, property developers made a substantial offer to buy the entirety of the land for development and in 2007 the land including the dwelling-house and sheds was sold for £2m.

One of the disputed issues was whether or not the large shed (which was 85 metres away from the house and which had been used throughout the period of ownership) was part of the main dwelling-house. After a detailed analysis of the main authorities on the definition of dwelling and curtilage, the FTT decided that whilst *Lady Rook* was a binding authority, it was "strictly irrelevant". The FTT seemed to arrive at this conclusion because in *Lady Rook* the Court considered a cottage occupied by a gardener which was 175 metres away and this was a different fact pattern to the one at hand.

The FTT preferred the decision in *Wakefield* and was content to disregard the "small curtilage" principles and apply the test of the "other" building being appurtenant to the "physical main building".

Applying the reasoning above, the FTT held that the shed was appurtenant to the main dwelling-house occupied by the Ritchie family and was therefore part of the dwelling-house.

It should be noted that HMRC have appealed the FTT decision in this case and that the Upper Tribunal will hear the full appeal on 6 and 7 November 2018.

Cases: *Batey (HMIT) v Wakefield* [1980] STC 572, [1980] TR 237, HC; *(HMIT) v Wakefield* [1981] STC 521, [1981] 55 TC 550, *CoA; Markey v Sanders* [1987] STC 256; 60 TC 245; *Williams v Merrylees* [1987] STC 445, 60 TC 297; *Dyer v Dorset County Council* [1989] 1 QB 346; *Lewis (HMIT) v Lady Rook* [1992] STC 171, 64 TC 567; *Ritchie & Ritchie v HMRC* [2017] UKFTT 449 (TC)

3.5.14   Other factors to take into account

Despite the authorities not mentioning the significance of conveyancing in determining whether a *residential* ancillary building is within the curtilage of a main dwelling-house, HMRC's manual at CG 64245 states that "buildings which are within the curtilage of a main house are also likely to pass on conveyance of that house without having to be specifically mentioned". Also at CG 64255, "a building which is appurtenant to the main house will also pass with it on conveyance without having to be specifically mentioned".

It is important to note at this stage that the term "curtilage" and its interpretation by the courts apply when establishing what constitutes part of a dwelling-house only (i.e. s. 222(1)(a)). It has no application when determining the permitted area of land used as a garden or grounds.

Guidance: CG 64245, CG 64255

3.6   Urban dwelling-houses and flats

Exactly two weeks after the Court of Appeal judgment in *Lady Rook* was handed down, the Chancery Division again considered and affirmed the single entity test. *Honour v Norris,* a case in which the taxpayer claimed main residence relief on the disposal of one of four flats in different buildings within the same London square arguing that they were part of the taxpayer's dwelling-house because they were occupied by the taxpayer and his family.

The flat in question was 60 and 80 yards away from the other flats and was used to provide accommodation for the taxpayer's elder children (from another marriage), accommodation for guests and occasional washing facilities and sleeping accommodation for the taxpayer and his spouse.

The General Commissioners agreed with the taxpayer that the flat in question could be considered part of his only or main residence as it constituted his dwelling-house. On an appeal by the Revenue, Vinellot J held that where flats in separate buildings are used to accommodate family members and guests, "it affronts common sense" to describe them as constituting a dwelling-house. The commissioners' findings of fact were inconsistent with their conclusion. For the learned judge, coming to a conclusion that the flat was part of the taxpayer's dwelling-house was the same as concluding that a house in a neighbouring village used for occasional personal use and for guests was part of the main dwelling-house in question.

Despite the favourable conclusion in *Norris*, HMRC's manual (CG 64305) currently concedes that:

> "There may be occasions where a group of flats can be considered to be one dwelling-house. This may be the case if they are

> - All occupied by the owner and his or her family
> - Within the same block
> - Contiguous.

> If the flats are in the same block but are on different floors or are separated by other flats, relief should only be allowed in exceptional circumstances. The length of occupation and the use of the flats are important factors in deciding how the flats should be treated and consideration should be given to all of the relevant facts and circumstances."

In terms of the factors to be considered when deciding if a group of flats can constitute a dwelling-house, it is hard to see how the length of occupation would make any difference if the flats are not all used by the same family or if they are physically separated. In the author's view, this is a concession that should be treated with caution in practice.

The position seems to be sufficiently clear with regards to a group of flats in the ownership and occupation of the same taxpayer (or even self-contained units within a house) being capable of constituting a "dwelling-house". Notwithstanding this, what happens when the flat has a garage or lock-up which is not physically attached to the block or which is not immediately contiguous to the flat in question? In this case, it seems a matter of proximity and conveyancing treatment. HMRC accept in their guidance (at CG 64292) that if the garage is "near" the residential accommodation and purchased and disposed of together but not within the curtilage of the building containing the flat it may still be treated as part of the dwelling-house. There is, however, no definition or guidance on the meaning of "near" and it is probably safe to assume that a few steps' walking distance would be sufficient to satisfy HMRC.

Case: *Honour (HMIT) v Norris* [1992] BTC 153
Guidance: CG 64305

3.7   Disposal of an "interest in" a dwelling-house

3.7.1   Meaning of "interest"

As well as giving relief (subject to conditions) for the disposal of a "dwelling-house", TCGA 1992, s. 222(1)(a) also refers to a disposal of an "interest in" a dwelling-house. For this reason, it may be worth exploring what an "interest" means for these purposes. It is safe to say that an interest in a dwelling-house will not be subject to a claim for main residence relief unless that interest can be disposed of for monetary value. It naturally follows, that unless an individual has a legal or equitable interest (with a respective value) in the relevant dwelling-house, or part of it, subsection (1)(a) will simply not apply.

According to the *Law of Property Act* 1925, s. 1(2), the only *legal interests* in or over land (those capable of subsisting or of being conveyed or created at law) are:

- easements, rights, or privileges in or over land for an interest equivalent to a legal estate (freehold or leasehold);
- rentcharges or charges on land which are perpetual or in the same terms as a freehold;
- mortgages;

- rights of entry exercisable over land under the terms of a freehold or annexed to a legal rentcharge.

All other interests in or over land take effect as *equitable interests*.

In a nutshell, main residence relief will be available on the disposal of a freehold, a long leasehold interest (in land law 21 years or more) as well as an interest in a minimal tenancy (short hold lease) in a dwelling-house. It therefore follows that if an individual occupies a dwelling-house as his main or only residence under a licence (even if contractual and in exchange for consideration), main residence relief will not be available as he will not hold a legal or equitable interest. This is significant in respect of elections under TCGA 1992, s. 222(5)(a) and the Revenue held a different view prior to 1994 which was withdrawn in a *Tax Bulletin* released in 1994. Transitional provisions apply for older elections (see **Chapter 8** below).

In the writer's view, and applying a common sense reading of the legislation, if an individual is resident in two dwelling-houses but holds no legal or equitable interest in respect of one, that dwelling-house should be ignored for the purposes of main residence relief. After all, if an individual occupies a second residence under a licence, he has no "interest in" it. For the less brave taxpayer, it would be important to consider the possibility of making an election that the dwelling-house which he owns or holds an interest in is treated as his main residence.

3.7.2   Joint ownership

"An interest" will also include a joint interest. Examples of joint ownership are a percentage interest in a dwelling owned under the shared ownership scheme (part buy/part rent) with a Housing Association, spouses or civil partners or unrelated people who own and occupy a dwelling as joint tenants (owning equal shares) or tenants in common (owning different shares according to their own monetary contribution). A disposal or deemed disposal of an interest or part of an interest by an individual who owns a residence jointly (and subject to the conditions and restrictions in TCGA 1992, Pt. VII – Private Residences) would therefore qualify for relief.

3.7.3   Tenants in common

Just like joint tenants, house owners or spouses/civil partners who are tenants in common will also benefit from a claim for main residence relief in respect of a disposal of their share of the interest in a "dwelling-house" (see **3.7.2** immediately above).

3.7.4   Leasehold interests – time limits

The legislation on main residence relief does not discriminate on grounds of ownership. Main residence relief is obtainable in respect of all leasehold interests. What this means is that an individual may be deemed to occupy a dwelling-house as his main residence even though he holds a very short lease or tenancy (monthly or even weekly) which would result in no capital gain (or negligible) in the event of a disposal. So, in reality, main residence relief would be available on the disposal (or deemed disposal) of a lease even though there is no taxable gain. This peculiarity in the legislation becomes significant when an individual owns more than one residence and does not realise the need to make an election pursuant to TCGA 1992, s. 222(5)(a). Strict time limits apply to any election and care should be taken (see **8.3.3** below).

3.7.5   Other interests

In cases where a tenant receives a capital sum from his landlord in exchange for vacating the "dwelling-house" which has been used as his main or only residence, or for not exercising his right to renew the lease, it seems as if this will be treated as a "sum derived from an asset" as defined by TCGA 1992, s. 22(1)(c):

> "(1)...there is for the purposes of this Act a disposal of assets by their owner where any capital sum is derived from assets notwithstanding that no asset is acquired by the person paying the capital sum, and this subsection applies in particular to—
>
> [...]
>
> (c) capital sums received in return for forfeiture or surrender of rights, or for refraining from exercising rights...".

Considering the wide scope of the legislation, it therefore follows that such a capital sum would be a disposal of an interest (short hold lease) in a "dwelling-house" as envisaged by TCGA 1992, s. 222(1)(a) and main residence relief would be available. According to established case law, if the capital sum is paid as a result of a statutory obligation imposed on the landlord then it would be outside the scope of CGT in any event. If, however, the capital sum is paid as part of an agreement or arrangement whereby the tenant's rights under the lease continue and are protected, then any surrender of rights is deemed to be a disposal for CGT purposes – *Davis v Powell* and *Drummond (HMIT) v Brown*).

HMRC's guidance at CG 64603 sets out a list of disposals and deemed disposals which may give rise to a "capital sum" derived from an interest in a dwelling-house. The manual includes the caveat that although main residence relief may be due in each of the cases listed, the conditions set out in the legislation must be met. The list appears as follows:

- the grant of a lease or sublease;
- the assignment of a lease;
- the surrender of a lease to the landlord;
- the surrender of rights of occupation by a tenant;
- the grant of an easement;
- the release of a restrictive covenant over neighbouring land;
- compensation or insurance monies for the destruction of the residence;
- the surrender of an interest in a co-ownership housing association;
- compensation or damages as a result of a cause of action.

The main factor in deciding whether main residence relief is available in the cases listed above is whether the right, easement, restrictive covenant, etc. is held by the individual as a direct consequence of ownership of the dwelling-house used as his main or only residence. If so, then the right is an "interest in" a dwelling-house and the capital sum derived from its (part) disposal.

Cases: *Davis v Powell* (1977) 51 TC 492; *Drummond (HMIT) v Brown* [1984] BTC 142

3.7.6 Gains that are not "interests in" a dwelling-house and which do not attract relief

According to HMRC's guidance at CG 64609, there are "assets" that although disposed of in connection with a residence, are not an interest in a residence. These are listed as follows:

- the disposal of a right to unascertainable future consideration received in consideration for a disposal of all or part of a residence, (a *Marren v Ingles* right);
- the disposal of shares in a company which owns a person's residence;
- the receipt of a forfeited deposit;
- the disposal of shares in a company set up by a residents association.

An error to avoid, when deciding if an asset disposed of amounted to an interest in a dwelling-house, is to assume that share stock in a company which owns a dwelling-house occupied as an individual's main or only residence amounts to an interest in a dwelling-house. This is quite a common mistake[6] because a shareholder does not and cannot own a legal or equitable interest in the company's assets. Care should be taken when advising clients who are non-domiciled and are tempted to hold UK residences through offshore corporate bodies/structures or (as HMRC point out in their manual) for companies incorporated to hold the freehold, the head lease or the legal interest in the common parts of a residential block of flats.

In that case, the residents will each hold a leasehold interest in their individual flat and shares in the company that owns the common parts. On the assignment or grant of a sub-lease, each resident will be entitled to main residence relief on his leasehold interest but no relief on his share in the company.

---

[6] Many members of the public believe that shareholders have the right to control the firm's assets and nearly four million internet search hits for the phrase "Shareholders are the owners of the company" illustrate the extent of the public misconception back in 2010.

3.8   Exchanges of interests in a dwelling-house

3.8.1   Different forms of exchange

An exchange of an interest in a residence may usually occur in one of two ways:

> First, joint owners of two properties may exchange their legal or equitable interests in order to own the separate and discrete dwelling which they occupy as their residence.

> Secondly, individuals who are sole owners of property may exchange their interests with or without further consideration. For these purposes, married couples and civil partners are treated as if they were a single individual.

The way in which an exchange of an interest in a dwelling-house is treated for CGT purposes (including roll over relief), and the availability of main residence relief, depend on whether the exchange happened before 6 April 2010, or whether it took place on or after that date.

3.8.2   Exchanges before 6 April 2010

Extra Statutory Concession ("ESC") D26 offers full relief on exchanges of private residences by joint owners in the following circumstances:

- when two or more joint owners exchange their interests in their respective residences in order to become sole owners;

- when each individual meets the conditions set out in TCGA 1992, s. 223 for main residence relief so that any gain in relation to the interest which they own in the dwelling-house would be exempt;

- where there is an undertaking by each individual that for CGT purposes he or she will acquire the other's interest in the dwelling-house, taking on the original base cost and the date of acquisition of the joint interest.

Example

Monica and Andrew are colleagues and flat mates. They work for the sales team at Big Buck Limited and had rented a flat in

63

Sunderland Block for many years. In 2002, as a result of record sales figures in Big Buck they both received a substantial end of year bonus and decided to invest jointly in the purchase of their Sunderland flat which was bought in November 2002 for £200,000. They continued to share their flat until 2006 when, after another successful year of sales, they jointly invested their bonuses in another flat in a similar block, Palace, which cost £250,000. Monica (who was now engaged) moved into it. In April 2009, as a result of her impending wedding, Monica agreed to exchange her interest in Sunderland for Andrew's share in Palace and because of the difference in the base cost of the properties she agreed to "bridge the gap" by paying an additional £30,000.

If Monica and Andrew disposed of their residences, then they would each be entitled to full main residence relief if they undertake that:

Andrew purchased Sunderland in 2002 for £200,000 and Monica purchased Palace in 2006 for £250,000. The additional payment of £30,000 is ignored for CGT purposes and forms no part of Monica's base cost.

3.8.3   Exchanges on or after 6 April 2010

For any disposals of joint interests, including exchanges, which occur on or after 6 April 2010, relief is given by way of a joint election for roll over relief pursuant to TCGA 1992, s. 248A-248E (see **9.2.5** for a discussion of the relationship between main residence relief and roll over relief).

Law: *Law of Property Act* 1925, s. 1(2); TCGA 1992, s. 22(1)(c), 222(1)(a), 222(5)(a), 248A-248E
Guidance: CG 64470, 64609; ESC D26

4. Gardens and grounds

4.1 Overview

In addition to relief on any gain made on the disposal of a dwelling-house used as a residence, s. 222(1)(b) also provides full relief from CGT on the disposal of adjoining land which an individual has for his own occupation and enjoyment with the said residence.

In so far as relevant, s. 222 provides relief for garden land or grounds as follows:

222. Relief on disposal of private residence

(1) This section applies to a gain accruing to an individual so far as attributable to the disposal of, or of an interest in–

[...] **or**

(b) **land** which he has for his own occupation and enjoyment with that residence as its **garden or grounds** up to the permitted area.

(2) In this section "**the permitted area**" means, subject to subsections (3) and (4) below, an area (inclusive of the site of the dwelling-house) of **0.5 of a hectare**.

(3) Where the area required for the **reasonable enjoyment** of the dwelling-house (or of the part in question) as a residence, having regard to the size and character of the dwelling-house, is larger than 0.5 of a hectare, that larger area shall be the permitted area.

(4) Where part of the land occupied with a residence is and part is not within subsection (1) above, then (up to the permitted area) that part shall be taken to be within subsection (1) above which, if the remainder were separately occupied, would be **the most suitable for occupation and enjoyment** with the residence.

In the past, a mistaken assumption has been made that the rules on main residence relief are the same for adjacent land and for the dwelling-house itself. There is a significant distinction between treatment in TCGA 1992 of a dwelling-house and of its garden land and it should be noted that s. 223 (amount of relief) applies to a disposal of a dwelling-house that has been – throughout the period of ownership – occupied as a main or only residence *and* of land which at the time of the disposal is occupied as garden or grounds up to the permitted area. All the other sections which comprise the *private residences* sections of TCGA 1992, Pt. VII refer to the dwelling-house only.

Section 222(1)(b) therefore reveals a test containing two limbs:

1. The land must be occupied as garden or grounds for the enjoyment of the residence.
2. The land must not exceed the "permitted area".

It should also be noted that even if land used as a garden or grounds meets the two conditions in the s. 222(1)(b) test, the amount of main residence relief will still be subject to all the other conditions in s. 223.

The draftsman deals with garden or grounds as a separate subsection in TCGA 1992, s. 222(1). This suggests that they are separate and should be distinctly considered from the main "dwelling-house" in question. It also means that an ancillary building, which is not within the curtilage of and appurtenant to the main house (a much more stringent test), may still qualify for main residence relief because it is situated within the permitted area of garden or grounds an individual has for his own occupation and enjoyment of his main residence.

4.2   What does "garden or grounds" include?

There is no definition of this phrase within the legislation or case law so its ordinary and natural meaning should apply. The Shorter *Oxford English Dictionary* defines "garden" as "a piece of ground (often enclosed) where fruits, flowers, herbs, or vegetables are cultivated; without specification esp. one adjoining a house or other residential building". "Grounds" are in turn defined as "a large enclosed area of land surrounding or attached to a house or other building".

The common characteristics between these two terms are a degree of enclosure (relevant to "permitted area" in this case) and an extent of physical attachment to the house.

It therefore follows that *gardens* may include vegetable patches, flower beds and pots, water features including ponds, extensive areas of lawn, and *grounds* may include fruit trees and orchards and less maintained areas like overgrown fields, meadows or paddocks (unless used commercially). As grounds are ordinarily defined as a larger enclosed area, it follows that any land developed into swimming pools, tennis courts or any other amenity areas may also qualify.

The determination of whether land amounts to a residence's garden or grounds is a matter of fact to be considered by the decision-maker on the specific circumstances of each case considering adequate historical data and any conveyances.

Generally speaking, it will be difficult (albeit not impossible) to establish that land which is physically separated from the main dwelling-house belongs to the house's garden or grounds just because it is in the ownership of the same individual. The crux of the argument would be that the land has to be occupied as grounds for the enjoyment of the residence. If the land is removed and not very easily accessible from the main house, enjoyment of it becomes a less likely possibility. A possible exception to this presumption would be gardens or grounds which are historically and traditionally separated from the dwelling-house because of local custom (e.g. historic villages with gardens across a footpath or highway).

Conversely, land which was previously occupied as gardens or grounds within the ordinary sense of the words, but which has been abandoned, is likely to fail the s. 222(1)(b) test due to lack of enjoyment at the time of disposal.

HMRC's guidance at CG 64360 explains that a useful dictionary definition for grounds (without mentioning which dictionary) would be:

> "Enclosed land surrounding or attached to a dwelling-house or other building serving chiefly for ornament or recreation."

HMRC seize upon the "enclosed" description of grounds without appreciating that there may be good reasons why gardens or grounds adequately occupied for the individual's enjoyment of the dwelling-house are not or could not be enclosed (restrictive covenants, planning conditions, etc.).

In the recent case of *Fountain v HMRC,* the FTT held that a gain accrued on a sale of a building plot located on land in the ownership of the appellants was not eligible for the exemption as the plot did not form part of the garden or grounds of their main residence.

The appellants lived in a residence at 31 Doddington Road for several years. They used an area behind the dwelling-house for business purposes (workshop and parking area). This area was accessed through a driveway on one side of the dwelling-house. There were two farming fields (of 1.31 and 1.80 acres respectively) beyond the business area. After cessation of the business, the appellants divided their land into five building plots. The issue for the FTT to determine was whether plot number 2 (which was sold in December 2009) formed part of the grounds or gardens of plot number 4, which had become a newly built dwelling-house and the appellants' main residence in January 2007.

The Tribunal found that plot 2 had been levelled and fenced off from the adjacent plots number 3 and number 4. The plot was said to have hard landscaping and was not cultivated. The appellants stated that it had been used for storing building materials used for the construction of the new main residence at plot 4 and for parking of a caravan, but no evidence was submitted to support this statement. Plots 2 and 4 were on the same "title deed" but they were physically separated by plot 3. There was no direct way of accessing plot 2 from the dwelling-house at plot 4.

The FTT held that following *Varty v Lynes*, the land in question had to form part of the garden or grounds of the main residence *at the time of the sale* (see **4.9.1** below). This meant that the fact (which was accepted) that plot 2 formed part of the grounds of the former residence at 31 Doddington Road was an irrelevant consideration.

Further, the fact that plots 2 and 4 were registered under the same title was also an irrelevant factor. In the FTT's view, the dictionary definition of "garden" contemplates that a garden should adjoin a residence and be cultivated as a garden. Plot 2 never adjoined plot 4 and there was no evidence that it had ever been cultivated as a garden, therefore it was not part of the garden of plot 4. Moreover, the dictionary definition of "grounds" contemplates that the land must surround a house or building and as plot 2 did not surround plot 4 and was physically separated by plot 3, it never formed part of the grounds of plot 4. Finally, the FTT held that the alleged fact (which was not proved) that plot 2 had been used for the storage of building materials and to park the appellants' caravan did not mean that the plot ever formed part of the garden or grounds of the main dwelling-house.

Cases: *Varty (HMIT) v Lynes* [1976] STC 508, (1976) 51 TC 419; *Fountain and Fountain v HMRC* [2015] UKFTT 0419 (TC)
Guidance: CG 64360

4.3 "Has for his occupation and enjoyment" – time of disposal

Section 222(1)(b) is phrased differently to its sister provision, s. 222(1)(a), in that it refers to the present tense and does not look back to periods of occupation over the length (or history) of ownership. This means that any land held as garden or grounds will not be required to be held contemporaneously with the dwelling-house if full main residence relief is to be obtained. If the land is held as garden or grounds at the date of disposal of the dwelling-house that would be, as a matter of legislative interpretation, sufficient.

Law: TCGA 1992, s. 222(1)(a), (b), s. 223

4.4 Permitted area – 0.5 ha or more if "reasonably required" for the enjoyment of the house

4.4.1 Introduction

Section 222(2) provides:

> "In this section "the permitted area" means, subject to subsections (3) and (4) below, an area (inclusive of the site of the dwelling-house) of 0.5 of a hectare."

The permitted area was originally set as one acre (by FA 1965) but in 1991, as a direct result of an EEC directive requiring the UK Government to stop using imperial measurements for most purposes by December 1994, FA 1991, s. 93 increased the permitted area by approximately 0.2 acres to half of a hectare. This change took effect from 19 March 1991 and the permitted area has been the same ever since.

It is ambiguous whether the use of the words "up to the permitted area" in s. 222(1)(b) is meant in the spatial or quantitative sense. The distinction is important because:

- If it was drafted and meant to be interpreted in its spatial sense, then it would mean that one would have to identify the physical boundaries of the permitted area first (which may exceed 0.5 ha) and then determine if the land sold was located within it. On this basis no relief would be due if the land sold was not within the boundaries of the permitted area even if it did not extend in itself beyond the permitted half a hectare.

- Conversely, if the section was meant to be read in a quantitative way, it would mean that any land which was enjoyed as garden or grounds which measured half a hectare or less would automatically qualify for relief. If this were the case, there would not be a requirement to look at the implications of s. 222(3) unless the area in question was, as a matter of fact, larger than 0.5 ha.

HMRC prefer the spatial reading of the provision (CG 64815) which imposes a burden on any house owner or landowner disposing of land used as a garden or grounds to identify the boundaries of the permitted area before and after any disposal.

There is a possibility[1] that when a large area in excess of the permitted area is going to be sold, more relief could be obtained on smaller consecutive transfers or part disposals than would be the case if the same total area were sold in one single transaction. For example, if the total area of grounds amounts to one hectare, the individual could dispose of the land in plots of 0.25 hectares or 0.5 hectares which, of course, would be covered by the permitted area exemption. The effectiveness of this route would be subject to the layout of the dwelling-house and whether the land disposed of can be described as the most suitable for occupation and enjoyment (for which expert opinion would be needed), to any anti-avoidance provisions or even to a finding that the transactions amount to a venture in the nature of a trade.

---

[1] The theory is treated as a possibility because each case may present factors and facts that could change the ultimate outcome or conclusion reached.

Subject to the potential pitfalls described above, in the author's view, there is nothing in the legislation that prevents main residence relief from being available in the sequential sale of land that has been occupied as a garden or grounds for the enjoyment of a dwelling-house.

4.4.2   Required for reasonable enjoyment

Half of a hectare is not a strict limit and the permitted area may be exceeded if "the area [is] required for the reasonable enjoyment of the dwelling-house (or of the part in question) as a residence" (TCGA 1992, s. 222(3)).

At first glance, the word "require" implies a subjective test which may be applied to the circumstances of a case bearing in mind the size and character of the adjoining dwelling-house. However, if the requirement was truly subjective in its absolute sense, every land owner would require their land for enjoyment of their dwelling-house, not the least because of the CGT savings. In the author's view, the words "reasonable enjoyment" which follow "required" render the test objective and the question for a fact-finding tribunal would be: would a reasonable landowner require all the land in question for the reasonable enjoyment of his dwelling-house?

It naturally follows that the larger the size of the house, the larger the plot of land which will be objectively required for the reasonable enjoyment of the house. Generally speaking property valuers would conclude – as a matter of good practice – that a house with a large footprint is likely to "deserve" a larger garden or grounds in the interest of privacy, space and general amenity. What follows is an analysis of the approach that the courts and HMRC have taken on this topic.

An interesting point to consider beforehand is that the legislation deliberately sets the permitted area at half of a hectare and therefore there is no discretion for an officer of HMRC to argue that it should be *smaller*, like for instance where the main dwelling-house is a small workers' cottage which either inherited or acquired enough land to bring its grounds to the relatively large area of half a hectare (or even larger if reasonably required).

Law: TCGA 1992, s. 222(1)(b), (2), (3), (4)
Guidance: CG 64815

71

4.4.3   *Longson – a subjective wish to enjoy a garden or grounds is not the correct test to be applied*

This view is supported by the decision of the High Court in the case of *Longson v Baker* where the taxpayer and his wife jointly bought Velmede Farm, which consisted of a substantial main house, several outbuildings, stables and an enclosed exercise yard which were laid out around a courtyard. The family had an interest in horses and had developed the site for that purpose. It was agreed by the Revenue that the dwelling-house included the stables.

Following a transfer on divorce from Dr Longson to his wife in 1995, the former Mrs Longson disposed of Velmede Farm in 1998 for development. The question for the General Commissioners to determine was whether the grounds amounting to just over seven and a half hectares were required for the reasonable enjoyment of the dwelling-house. The Commissioners dismissed the appeal and found that whilst convenient or desirable for the taxpayer to have the land, seven and a half hectares were "not required for the reasonable enjoyment of Velmede Farm as a residence, having regard to it's [sic] size and character". On appeal by the taxpayer to the High Court, Evans-Lombe J dismissed the appeal holding that:

> "It is clear from the words 'required for the reasonable enjoyment' in subsection (3), that the test to be applied as to what any larger permitted area can consist of over the 0.5 hectares allowed by the section, is an objective test. In my judgment it is not objectively required, i.e. necessary, to keep horses at a house in order to enjoy it as a residence. An individual taxpayer may subjectively wish to do so but that is not the same thing."

Case: *Longson v Baker* (HMIT) [2001] STC 6, [2001] BTC 356

4.4.4   *Newhill – "required" for the amenity or convenience of any house*

In coming to its decision in *Longson*, the High Court was persuaded by *obiter dicta* in the compulsory purchase case of *Re Newhill Compulsory Purchase Order* and by what could be described as a policy decision by the Court. Evans-Lombe J was persuaded that if the taxpayer's appeal were to be allowed, "there will be a substantial increase in the demand for horses amongst the owners of houses with grounds which have development potential [and] ... this cannot have been the statutory purpose of the legislature in legislating section 222 subsection (3)".

Endorsing the comparison made[2] between an objection against a compulsory purchase order and a decision on the extent of gardens or grounds for main residence relief constituted a significant misunderstanding by the High Court of the *Newhill* case. By way of background, for the purposes of *Newhill,* the *Housing Act* 1936, s. 75 provided that:

> "Nothing in this Act shall authorise the compulsory acquisition for the purposes of this part of this Act of **any land, which** at the date of the compulsory purchase order, **forms part of any** park, **garden, or pleasure ground or is otherwise required** for the amenity or convenience of any house" (emphasis added).

In other words, the legislation dealt with land which did *not* fall within a park, garden or "pleasure" ground of a dwelling (which in turn could not be compulsorily acquired by a local planning authority), so the question to be determined was whether this type of land would be required for the amenity or convenience of any house despite not being "recreational" land. The test in s. 222(3) establishes whether land which is already "recreational" is occupied as a garden. The nuance between housing legislation and TCGA 1992 is significant and was unfortunately overlooked by the Court in *Newhill.*

This point was clarified by the Court of Appeal a year later in *Re Ripon (Highfield) Housing Confirmation Order* when it was held that the decision on the question whether the particular land is part of a park or not is preliminary to the exercise of the jurisdiction to make and confirm an order. If the decision was that the land was part of a park, no order could be made and the question of amenity and convenience would be inconsequential.

This is in direct contradiction to the provision at TCGA 1992, s. 222(1)(b) where the decision-maker must establish whether land which falls within the garden or grounds of a house is reasonably required for the enjoyment of the dwelling-house.

---

2 By the District Valuer and the General Commissioners.

Taxpayers and their advisers should therefore be wary of accepting arguments which rely exclusively on the decision in *Newhill* as the "analogy" drawn by the Court in that case is not as helpful as it is believed by HMRC.

Recently, in *Ritchie & Ritchie*, the FTT had the benefit of an expert report and comparables from the District Valuer which suggested that the permitted area for a three-storey dwelling-house just outside of Moneymore, Co. Londonderry was (or should be) 4,967.58 m² (and the rest is 1,625.75m²) (see **3.5.13** above). The District Valuer accepted that even if the large shed was part of the dwelling-house (which the FTT held it was) then the permitted area would be 0.5ha. The Appellants submitted a report from Savills (but did not present an expert for cross-examination) that the excess over the permitted area should be 0.05ha.

The FTT considered all the evidence but came to its own conclusion. On the basis that the large shed was part of the dwelling-house they included a loop of land surrounding the house, gardens and shed but disallowed all of the land to the east (including the land to the north of the shed) and the land south of the shed, on the basis that it was not required (or necessary) for the use or enjoyment of the shed. Nor was the land to the west of the shed that lied south of a line extending from the front of the shed to the western boundary of the land. The excess land over the permitted area was therefore 0.1ha (or one seventh of the total area of the site: 0.699ha).

For the FTT's conclusion on apportionment of the gain for the period before occupation see **4.8.3** below.

Law: *Housing Act* 1936, s. 75; TCGA 1992, s. 222(1)(b), (3)
Cases: *Re Newhill Compulsory Purchase Order 1937, Paynes Application* [1938] 2 All ER 163; *Re Ripon (Highfield) Housing Confirmation Order 1938, White and Collins v Minister of Health* [1939] 2 KB 838, [1939] 3 All ER 548; *Ritchie & Ritchie v HMRC* [2017] UKFTT 449 (TC)

4.5 HMRC's guidance on "permitted area"

HMRC's manuals starting at CG 64800 refer to the determination of the extent of the permitted area to be one of the most common areas of disagreement with taxpayers. HMRC rely heavily on the Office of the District Valuer to advise both on the extent and location of the permitted area.

The manual instructs officers on the procedure for dealing with and challenging claims for inclusion within the permitted area or claims for a larger permitted area.

As explained in the guidance, in order to determine the extent of the permitted area, an officer must first decide:

- the extent of the entity of the dwelling-house (considered very important);
- the extent to which that dwelling-house has been used as a residence (see **2.2** above); and
- the extent of the garden and grounds.

Where land (including the dwelling-house) occupied as a garden or grounds does not exceed half a hectare, relief will apply automatically. Exceptions to this rule include disposals of garden or grounds after a disposal of the dwelling-house and if part of the half hectare of land was not, as a matter of fact, occupied as a garden or grounds.

When making a determination, the District Valuer will consider three factors:

- first, the size and character of the dwelling-house;
- second, what part of the dwelling-house has been used as its owner's residence; and
- third, what land is required for the reasonable enjoyment of that residence.

In the author's view, the second factor listed above misses the cogent decision in *Green v IRC*. In that case, the Court rejected as "startling" a Revenue argument that a part of the main dwelling-house which was not used or occupied (because the house was larger than the household required) did not form part of the dwelling-house. The High Court held that although the mansion house had 33 rooms, it was still occupied as the dwelling-house and main residence of the taxpayer and his immediate family. The second factor is also highly "subjective" and overlooks the fact that the test for reasonable enjoyment is objective and whilst some areas of the main house may not be used by that particular taxpayer and/or family (and therefore a smaller area of garden or grounds may seem to be required for the enjoyment of the dwelling), a reasonable bystander may still conclude that the land is required for the reasonable enjoyment of the dwelling-house as a whole.

If part of the garden or grounds of a residence is not strictly used or enjoyed with that residence but does not exceed the permitted area (0.5 ha), that part may be treated as being "up to the permitted area" if the part which is used as a garden would be the "most suitable for occupation and enjoyment with the residence" if it were separately occupied (TCGA 1992, s. 222(4)). This is said to be a question of location on a particular site and a question to be decided by the District Valuer.

In cases where there is more than one disposal of land, the permitted area determination will need to be made at the date of each disposal as the permitted area for the same dwelling-house may change if:

- there is a change in the size or character of the dwelling-house: this could result in an increase or decrease in the permitted area;
- the trend in the post-war years for smaller gardens (because of the cost and inconvenience of maintaining a large garden) continues: the amount of land required when a house was built may be too large today;
- a house located in an area which was historically rural and then becomes "urbanised": the dwelling-house may be left with anomalously large grounds as gardens in rural areas tend to be larger than in urban areas.

The permitted area available on a second disposal is not reduced by the area of land subject to main residence relief in the first disposal.

The separate disposal of land within the garden or grounds of a dwelling-house creates a rebuttable presumption that this particular area of land was not reasonably required for the enjoyment of the main dwelling-house.

Law: TCGA 1992, s. 222(2), (3), (4)
Case: *Green v CIR* [1982] BTC 378
Guidance: CG 64800ff.

4.6 Distance, separation, location

HMRC's guidance at CG 64367 tells officers that they should strongly resist any taxpayer argument that land which is separated from the main dwelling-house by a physical boundary or land in third party ownership should be allowed as part of the garden or grounds because it is in common ownership. Whilst it is true that the mere fact that land is within the same ownership is insufficient to determine that the land belongs to the garden or grounds of a dwelling-house, separation is not a definite block to relief in appropriate cases.

The real test to be applied is whether the land is being occupied and enjoyed by the main dwelling-house as a garden or grounds. The Revenue (in *Tax Bulletin* 18, August 1995) construct "occupation" and "enjoyment" using the legal meaning of the words: "Occupation means possession of the land while enjoyment means possession without contested claims from third parties". Plainly, this expressed view means that there is no need for actual use or conventional enjoyment of the land and unkept or overgrown areas of land will still qualify subject to the other conditions. This also means that gardens which are not exclusively in use for recreational purposes may be able to benefit from the exemption too.

Example

Mr and Mrs Bagshott own a substantial dwelling-house with a historical garden and a large paddock which was bought by Mr Bagshott's grandfather in 1930 and inherited by Mr Bagshott. Both Mr and Mrs Bagshott are keen gardeners and use the paddock during fair weather. The local horticultural society uses the gardens for research from time to time for a small "entry fee". The fact that the gardens are used by the horticultural society does not prevent the gardens from qualifying for relief if all other conditions are met.

There may be cases where, for historical (or other) reasons, a dwelling-house has the benefit of a small area of land immediately to the back followed by a substantial garden across a water course, footpath, bridleway or road. If the owner is able to show that such a plot of land is used and enjoyed as the house's gardens/grounds (i.e. there are plants, trees, flowers, herbs, water features and there is space for small animals grazing, stables, etc.) then the fact that it is not immediately adjacent to the dwelling-house should not be an impediment for s. 222(1)(b) or (3) to apply, in particular if the entire property including the two separate plots of land would be conveyed together.

Indeed, in the case of *Wakeling v Pearce,* where the landowner inherited a bungalow and a field approximately 10 yards away, which were separated by a cottage in third-party ownership, the taxpayer sold the field in two separate plots and claimed main residence relief on the basis that this field was occupied and enjoyed as a garden. HMRC resisted the claim but the Special Commissioners found, after testing the taxpayer's evidence, that the field had been used for many years as part of her "garden or grounds".

The Revenue stated in their *Tax Bulletin* 18 (August 1995) that: "the Revenue has decided not to test the matter in the High Court due to her particular circumstances. The facts of the case and the decision do not affect the Revenue's interpretation of this Section" (i.e. s. 222(1)(b)). This particular section of the *Tax Bulletin* (or *Revenue Interpretation*) did not make it to their subsequent manual at CG 64367 or anywhere else for that matter. Inferences could be drawn from the fact that the Revenue consciously decided it would not be helpful to mention the decision to taxpayers.

Notwithstanding *Wakeling,* and as a matter of common sense, a substantial distance from the dwelling-house could negate the argument that a plot of land is used as a garden or grounds; after all, it is a garden[3] that the legislation specifies, not an allotment or any other type of land.

As with many questions relating to main residence relief, it is always a matter of fact and each case will inevitably turn on its own facts.

Law: TCGA 1992, s. 222(1)(b), (3)
Case: *Wakeling v Pearce* (1995) SpC 32
Guidance: CG 64367; *Tax Bulletin* 18, August 1995

---

[3] Within its ordinary meaning.

4.7   Part disposal of land used as gardens or grounds

4.7.1   Generally

As the population of urban areas and suburban areas grows and the demand for single-person households increases, the desirability of selling land with development value has significantly increased in the last decade. This means that a number of landowners are selling off parts of their gardens and grounds (in particular if they are larger than 0.5 ha) in exchange for substantial sums of capital. Naturally, every owner would wish to avoid paying CGT on the disposal of such land and this has become the most common cause of disputes with HMRC.

HMRC's argument (as set out in their Guidance at CG 64832) is that the part disposal of land (in particular in cases where there is planning permission granted or a substantial development value) used as gardens or grounds creates a rebuttable presumption that the land was not reasonably required for the enjoyment of the dwelling-house as a residence in the first instance. HMRC officers tend to argue (in most cases supported by the Office of the District Valuer) that the increasing housing demand has led to a reduction in the sizes of garden plots (in particular in urban and suburban areas) and that as a consequence larger gardens are no longer "required" for the amenity and convenience of a dwelling-house in this type of location. Where a house owner disposes of part of his garden or grounds and remains in occupation of the dwelling-house, the logic of this contention would be harder to resist. Although there is some strength in HMRC's argument, it should also be considered that there may be good reasons (financial or otherwise) why someone would decide to part with their "garden" and that s. 222(3) is not drafted in absolute terms and the wording of the section does not exclude this type of disposal from relief.

For example, in a case where a property owner disposes of a significant part of the grounds surrounding his dwelling-house, and where planning permission has been granted for the development of that part of the land for residential use, there will be an inevitable reduction in the dwelling's value and a "conversion" of land as a capital asset into a sum of money. Depending on the size and context of the dwelling-house and its grounds, and on the amount of land sold to a third party, the dwelling-house may well lose desirability as a private residence (because of resulting noise, reduced tranquillity or high-density development in its proximity). The marketability of the house, and/or its future use, is an entirely separate matter to the identification of the "extended" permitted area at the time of the disposal as envisaged by s. 222(3). The question to be considered pursuant to s. 222(3) is whether the part of the grounds which has been sold – at the time of the disposal – was reasonably required for the enjoyment of the particular dwelling-house.

Any cash consideration received for the part disposal of garden land should (in most cases) be treated as compensation to the owner for any loss of "amenity" or "convenience" not as proof that the land was not required for the enjoyment of the dwelling at the time of disposal.

This position may prove more difficult to defend in cases where the part of the grounds sold was purchased after the acquisition of the main dwelling-house, in particular if the land is held for a relatively limited period of time (and there may also be a risk of an assessment for trading income).

Notwithstanding this, in the author's view (and in particular in cases where the garden does not exceed 0.5 ha), HMRC's arguments should not be taken at face value and a challenge should be considered in certain cases.

HMRC correctly recognise at CG 64832 that there may be situations where the presumption that garden land sold in a part disposal was not "reasonably required" should not apply, and give as an example:

- A disposal of part of the garden and grounds within the family. In these circumstances the owner may be prepared to tolerate some curtailment of the reasonable enjoyment of his or her own residence.
- A disposal of part of the garden and grounds due to financial necessity. Financial difficulties may force a person to dispose of a piece of land which would otherwise be regarded as part of the garden and grounds required for the reasonable enjoyment of the residence.

Law: TCGA 1992, s. 222(3)
Guidance: CG 64832

4.7.2 *Mitigating CGT on a part disposal – planning tips*

In cases where it would be difficult to show that the land disposed of was reasonably required for the enjoyment of the dwelling-house, a possible answer would be to incorporate the land fully into the land owner's domain by using it and occupying it as a garden (planting, landscaping, etc.), and to dispose of land which was part of the original title (and within the permitted area) before or instead of the newly-acquired plot. If the position on the ground permits it, the new land may then be treated as the new permitted area at a subsequent sale of the dwelling-house.

A possible way of mitigating an inevitable CGT charge would be to plan well ahead of the part disposal and consider making a no gain, no loss gift to a spouse/civil partner with a lower income who may be able to benefit from the 18% CGT rate (for residential property) and a further annual exempt amount and who may potentially have current or brought forward capital losses.

If the plans to sell are not in the near future, the owner may consider transferring the land in question into a trust which allows occupation of the land as a life tenant. There would be no capital gain on the original transfer (and there would be a lifetime chargeable transfer at a reduced IHT rate of 20% on the value of assets above the nil-rate band) and depending on the period of time it is held on trust, there should be relatively modest gains on a future disposal. The land would have to be (or be capable of being shown as being) the "most suitable for occupation and enjoyment with the residence"; that being the case, main residence relief may be available pursuant to s. 222(1)(b).

Landowners and advisers should be aware that HMRC might challenge such a claim for relief on the basis that the provisions envisage one exemption per disposal only and that this type of trust settlement goes beyond the intention of Parliament. This argument could be resisted by insisting on a purposive and pragmatic reading of the legislation: s. 222(1)(b) grants exemption from CGT to a disposal of garden land, or part of it, and a transfer into a trust would be doing just that. Trusts can be complex and legal advice should be sought before settling any trust.

A more extreme way of mitigating or avoiding a CGT charge completely (in particular in cases where there is a significant development value in the grounds and where there is a need to downsize) would be to dispose of the entire plot of land including the dwelling-house to a potential developer or willing purchaser. If the land containing the house's gardens and grounds has been occupied and enjoyed accordingly, there would be a stronger case to make that it fell within the permitted area in its entirety. Any tax issues as to a future disposal or demolition of the dwelling-house would then be shifted to the new owners (if they so wish). This option would obviously depend on how attached to the house the landowners are, how much is the development value of the land and the amount of time available before a sale in order to embark upon effective planning.

4.8 Land owned before the dwelling-house

4.8.1 Generally

As discussed at **4.3**, TCGA 1992, s. 222(1)(b) does not oblige the owner of a "dwelling-house" to have owned and occupied garden land simultaneously with the main dwelling-house. As long as the garden or grounds (up to the permitted area) are occupied as such at the time of sale, main residence relief is in principle available.

If land occupied as a garden or grounds at the time of disposal was also held as a bare plot of land before the dwelling-house was constructed, there may be a need to adjust any relief available to reflect the period of time during which the land was not part of the individual's main or only residence.

In cases where land was owned for a relatively short period of time, Extra-Statutory Concession D49 may be invoked to bridge the time gap (see **6.6.8** below).

The position gets a bit more complicated where an individual buys a substantial plot of land, obtains planning permission to build a dwelling-house which he then occupies as his main residence *and* subsequently divides the garden into plots which are then sold for further development.

This was the situation, more or less, in the *Henke* case.

4.8.2 Henke & Henke – land owned before construction of the dwelling-house, apportionment of expenditure and proceeds, and permitted area

In an appeal to the Special Commissioners heard in 2006 in which the taxpayer (Mr Anthony Henke) represented himself and his wife, there were several issues for the Commissioners to adjudicate upon:

(1) the validity of discovery assessments made in respect of the year 1999-2000;

(2) the validity of the enquiry into their 2000-01 self-assessment returns;

(3) the costs to be allowed against the sale proceeds from each plot in the computation of the chargeable gains;

(4) the size and location of the "permitted area" in relation to the residence;

(5) whether any main residence relief in relation to the sales of each plot needed to be restricted to exclude the period between the date when the land was acquired and the date on which the house became their only or main residence.

The commentary that follows will refer to points (3) to (5) as these are the most relevant for present purposes.

Summary of facts

Mr and Mrs Henke jointly purchased the freehold of a plot of land in Huntingdon in August 1982. After a fencing exercise, the plot was found to consist of 2.66 acres and the local planning authority granted conditional outline permission for the construction of one dwelling-house only. Detailed planning permission was obtained in February 1991 which approved the design of a house now known as Old Oak House and a landscaping scheme for the entire 2.66 acres of land.

The planning restriction was lifted in December 1991 with the effect of allowing further planning permission applications to be made if so desired. Old Oak House was completed in June 1993, at which time Mr and Mrs Henke moved in and occupied it as their main residence. Old Oak House was substantial in size with 4,500 square feet of living accommodation and an adjacent garage block of 1,000 square feet.

Two plots of 0.54 acres each were sold by Mr and Mrs Henke in 1999 and 2001 respectively. The two plots had the benefit of planning permission (granted in 1995) for the construction of two dwelling-houses and had been maintained as part of Old Oak House's grounds up until the time of disposal.

The parties' arguments

The taxpayers argued that the plots sold were required for the enjoyment of Old Oak House as a residence and that they were entitled to full main residence relief. The District Valuer (who presented an expert report) disagreed with this contention and opined "that he did not believe that the property 'required' 2.66 acres for its reasonable enjoyment. He attached a plan showing the area that he considered to be 'required'. This area was 2.03 acres; he described this remaining area, after the removal of the two former 'meadow' areas, as 'generous'."

In addition, the taxpayers argued that the "period of ownership" included the time since they had purchased the plot of land in 1982 so that no apportionment would be needed to effect main residence relief. The Revenue disagreed with this contention, arguing that the term "period of ownership" related to the asset (the land) and not the dwelling-house. This interpretation would amount to adopting a purposive approach to the legislation.

The Commissioner's decision

Main residence relief in principle

The Special Commissioner, Mr Clark, held that it could not be argued that Old Oak had not been the taxpayers' main residence since they started to live in it in 1993. However, the taxpayers were not entitled to main residence relief for the period of ownership *before* the residence existed on the ground. This meant that an apportionment had to be made pursuant to TCGA 1992, s. 223(2).

Costs allowable against sales proceeds

One more apportionment had to be made in respect of the expenditure incurred on the dwelling-house and another on the expenditure incurred on the plots sold. Relying on TCGA 1992, s. 42, Mr Clark concluded that:

> "unless any of the expenditure on building Old Oak House and its garage can be regarded as having been reflected in either or both of Plot 1 and Plot 2, it cannot be taken into account under s 38 TCGA 1992 as an allowable deduction in computing the gains on the sale of those plots".

Permitted area

As noted by the Special Commissioner, in the absence of any expert evidence adduced by the taxpayers, he had no choice but to accept the expert evidence of the District Valuer that the permitted area consisted of 2.03 acres. According to the District Valuer (and the Commissioner agreed) this was more generous than the maximum of 0.5 ha or 1.24 acres and it was justified under TCGA 1992, s. 222(1)(b) taking into account the house's location and size and "comparable properties" in the area.

The apportionment of the sale proceeds between the land which fell within the permitted area and the land which fell outside it would be based on the size of the plots and the permitted *area* and not on the value of sale proceeds and the remaining interests. This approach would stay true to the "permitted area" decision and circumvent a reference to the Lands Tribunal on matters of land valuation.

The period of ownership

Mr Clark remarked that despite the CGT legislation being in place since 1965, there were no reported decisions on the meaning of "period of ownership" within s. 222. In the circumstances, the Commissioner decided that:

> "The Parliamentary intention behind the legislation is clear; there is to be only one period of ownership, of the single asset consisting of the land and any buildings which may be erected on it during that period. It follows that an apportionment is required where land is held for a period and subsequently a house is built on it and occupied as the individual's only or main residence."

This decision highlights two important considerations for landowners and house owners to take into account before the sale of land occupied as a garden or grounds.

Law: TCGA 1992, s. 222(1)(b), s. 223(2)

Case: *Henke v HMRC* (2006) SpC 550

4.8.3   *Ritchie & Ritchie – the FTT disagrees with Henke's apportionment principles*

Mr and Mrs Ritchie bought 0.669 hectares of land just outside of Moneymore, Co. Londonderry in 1987. The land purchased was part of the old dismantled train station and railway line. There were two buildings present on the land, a large shed which had stood on the old western platform and a small "potting" shed. The Ritchie family used the large shed (or garage) to store children's toys, the family car, various tools, firewood and vegetables and also the ploughs which the husband used in ploughing competitions.

During construction, the Ritchie family rented another house bordering the land and laid a path that led to the shed. They obtained planning permission in 1991, built a substantial three-storey house together with front and back gardens and moved in 1995. In June 2006, property developers made a substantial offer to buy the entire site for development and in 2007 the land including the dwelling-house and sheds were sold for £2m. There was, therefore, a pre-occupation period of seven years before *a* dwelling-house was constructed on the site.

The FTT considered whether the capital gain should be time apportioned because – as HMRC argued – the asset was changed substantially because of the construction of the house. The taxpayers argued that the large shed had been part of the dwelling rented by the taxpayers throughout the pre-occupation period and which was linked by a path.

The FTT rejected the taxpayers' argument that the shed was part of their main residence located on somebody else's land and found support for this finding by the absence of an election treating the shed as their main residence (mostly because it had not been occupied as such).

Despite the above finding, the FTT found it difficult to time apportion the gain as per *Henke* (which is not a binding authority in any event). If a time apportionment had been made, 35% of an approximate gain of £1.8m would have to be disallowed. The FTT held that "by no yardstick" had the land increased in value by £630,000 in a seven-year gap. Instead, the FTT proceeded to apportion according to the principles in s. 224(2):

> "(2) If at any time in the period of ownership there is a change in what is occupied as the individual's residence, whether on account of a reconstruction or conversion of a building *or for any other reason*, or there have been changes as regards the use of part of the dwelling house for the purpose of a trade or business, or of a profession or vocation, or for any other purpose, the relief given by section 223 *may be adjusted in a manner which is just and reasonable.*" (Emphasis added).

The FTT found that it would not stretch impermissibly the wording of the provision if they looked at the factual situation in the Ritchies' case as a change in what was occupied as a residence for "any other reason" and not necessarily a reconstruction or conversion.

The FTT applied s. 224(2) so that the gains reflected the value of the dwelling-house in early 1995 (£200,000) from which they deducted the agreed cost of construction (deductible under TCGA 1992, s. 38) of £179,900 and the cost of the land of £11,000. The total disallowable gain was therefore £9,100.

It should be noted that HMRC have appealed the FTT decision in this case and that the Upper Tribunal will hear the full appeal on 6 and 7 November 2018.

Law: TCGA 1992, s. 38, 223(2), 224(2)

Case: *Ritchie v Ritchie v HMRC* [2017] UKFTT 449 (TC)

4.9 Land retained and sold after the dwelling-house – timing of sale

4.9.1 *Varty v Lynes – land must be occupied as a garden or grounds at the time of disposal*

Whilst main residence relief may be obtained (subject to the restrictions highlighted above) on land which was owned before the dwelling-house, the opposite is true in respect of land which remains in the taxpayer's ownership after a disposal of his main residence.

The leading case on this point is *Varty v Lynes,* an appeal by way of case stated by the Revenue from a decision by the General Commissioners allowing main residence relief on the disposal of garden land made after a disposal of the dwelling-house. The taxpayer, Mr Lynes, bought a house and garden in Sussex in 1968 for £6,920. The total area of the land including the garden was less than an acre (so no dispute over spatial permitted area was in point). The dwelling-house and the garden were occupied as Mr Lynes' main residence until he sold the house and a part of the garden in 1971 for £10,000. He retained the remainder of the land and applied for outline planning permission which he obtained in January 1972. The remaining land was then sold with the benefit of planning permission a few months later for £10,000.

The taxpayer argued that the exemption afforded by FA 1965, s. 29 (the predecessor to TCGA 1992, s. 222) was equally available whether the dwelling-house and garden were sold off in the course of one or two separate transactions.

In allowing this argument, the General Commissioners placed great weight on the last part of s. 29(2) which read:

> "The gain shall not be a chargeable gain if the dwelling-house or part ... has been the individual's only or main residence throughout the period of ownership ... except ... for the last 12 months of that period."

Brightman J. explored the anomalies that could be said to exist if either of the parties' interpretation of the legislation was allowed to stand. For instance, on the Revenue's construction, the exception for the purposes of s. 29(2) of the last 12 months of the period of ownership in respect of the dwelling-house should also apply to the garden/grounds. Another "comparable anomaly" would also arise under s. 29(3) where one must make an apportionment on a time basis in relation to the dwelling-house. On the taxpayer's construction of the section, it would mean that a taxpayer who disposes of his dwelling-house, and then two decades later disposes of his garden, would still be able to benefit from the exemption.

The learned judge found it difficult to relate the expression "land which he has for his own occupation and enjoyment with that residence as its garden or grounds" to anything but the actual time of disposal in circumstances where s. 29(1)(a) is clearly looking both to the present and the past whilst by direct contrast s. 29(1)(b) is looking to the present only.

It was therefore held that – despite anomalies and possible injustices – land retained after a sale of the main dwelling-house could not benefit from main residence relief on a subsequent disposal.

Law: FA 1965, s. 29(1), (2); TCGA 1992, s. 222(1)(b)
Case: *Varty (HMIT) v Lynes* [1976] STC 508, (1976) 51 TC 419

4.9.2 *Dickinson – relief may continue to be due even if development on grounds has already started*

The more recent case of *Dickinson* shows that main residence relief can continue to be available even if construction works had started on garden land by the date of the disposal of the dwelling-house.

In this case, the taxpayer owned a substantial dwelling-house in Lincolnshire and a large garden and grounds which included a tennis court.

In 2007, 0.16 ha of the garden (part of the tennis court) was sold to a company of which the taxpayer was a director. The land was disposed of to make way for the development of four dwelling-houses. The start date of the development was agreed by the board of the company to be Easter of 2007. The terms of the conveyance were that the taxpayer would not receive any consideration until such time as each of the new dwelling-houses was completed and sold. Despite an unsigned draft contract being in existence, the company was (erroneously) given permission to start building work for the development and did so on 7 June 2007.

After a delay caused by issues with an access road which had not been adopted as a public highway by the local county council, contracts were formally exchanged on 27 July 2007. The taxpayer did not declare the sale proceeds on her tax return on the basis that she was entitled to main residence relief on the entire proceeds. HMRC resisted on the ground that as the land was under development at the date of contract, it was not available to the taxpayer as "garden or grounds".

The First-tier Tribunal held that the expression "garden or grounds" in s. 222(1)(b) must be given its ordinary everyday meaning. In order for a garden or grounds to lose their inherent character, any change must be permanent or capable of being regarded as permanent. The change cannot be transient or conditional. As the company had been given permission to start building foundations on an informal basis only, the permission to build did not constitute a disposal of the land. The land had retained its character as "garden or grounds" within the meaning of the legislation until the actual time of disposal in July 2007 when contracts had been formally exchanged.

Law: TCGA 1992, s. 222(1)(b)

Case: *Dickinson v HMRC* [2013] UKFTT 653 (TC)

4.10 Shared gardens or grounds and "splitting" land

Questions of proximity, of occupation and of whether the permitted area may be extended (by showing that depriving the residence of a larger area of land would lead to real injury to the enjoyment of the owner) tend to arise more often in cases of substantial country estates with large dwelling-houses and extensive grounds.

In practice, additional questions arise when there is more than one dwelling-house occupying and sharing the use of the garden or surrounding grounds. This is referred to as holding an interest in land in "undivided shares". The term "undivided shares" connotes that a common area of gardens or grounds has not been parcelled or separated to the exclusion of others. An example of this situation would be a mansion house with substantive gardens which is converted into several flats each sharing the use of the grounds equally.

For land valuation purposes, the asset to be valued would be the individual owner's interest in the grounds which is subject to the rights of others. In order to determine (or even contend) the value of the permitted area in respect of one of those dwellings – and because an undivided share of a garden is less marketable than an entire interest – the valuation would have to be significantly reduced to reflect the "restricted" interest.

A possible solution would be to split the land into parcels of up to half a hectare (ensuring that the plans attached to the land registry are amended accordingly) and at the same time grant each dwelling an easement or right of entry/access to the entire area of the formerly shared gardens.

Guidance: CG 74243

5. Job-related living accommodation

5.1 Effect of relief

222 (8)

> If at any time during an individual's period of ownership of a dwelling-house or part of a dwelling-house he–
>
> (a) resides in living accommodation which is for him job-related, and
>
> (b) intends in due course to occupy the dwelling-house or part of a dwelling-house as his only or main residence,
>
> this section and sections 223 to 226 shall apply as if the dwelling-house or part of a dwelling-house were at that time occupied by him as a residence.

Main residence relief is also available for an individual who owns a dwelling-house but has to reside in job-related living accommodation. The effect of this provision is to treat the dwelling-house or part thereof as if it were at the time occupied as a *residence.* It should be noted that this extension does not automatically deem the dwelling to be a main residence and an election may therefore be advisable (see **5.4** below).

The conditions for this extension of the relief are twofold:

First, the accommodation must be "job-related" (see **5.2.2** below).

Second, the individual must intend to occupy his dwelling-house as his only or main residence in due course. This is considered at **5.3** below.

Law: TCGA 1992, s. 222(8)

5.2 Who is likely to benefit

5.2.1 Overview

TCGA 1992, s. 222(8A) distinguishes between three types of individuals:

- employees;
- the self-employed; and
- company directors.

Each of these is considered below.

5.2.2   *Employees*

Section 222(8A)(a) defines "job-related living accommodation" in the same terms as for the benefits in kind provisions in ITEPA 2003, Pt. 3, Ch. 5. It means accommodation provided to an employee (or to his spouse or civil partner) by reason of his employment in any of the following cases:

i.   where it is necessary for the proper performance of the duties of the employment that the employee should reside in that accommodation;

ii.   where the accommodation is provided for the better performance of the duties of the employment, and it is customary for employers to provide living accommodation to employees; or

iii.   where the accommodation is provided as part of arrangements that deal with or prevent a security threat.

These three cases are considered in turn below.

Proper performance

HMRC accept at EIM 11342 that the following employees satisfy the "necessary for proper performance of the duties" test.

- agricultural workers who live on farms or agricultural estates;
- lock-gate and level-crossing gate keepers;
- full-time caretakers living on the premises;
- stewards and green keepers living on the premises;
- wardens of sheltered housing schemes living on the premises where they are on call outside normal working hours;

Better performance and customary

HMRC explain at EIM 11347 that as the term "customary" is not defined in statute, it should take its ordinary meaning. According to their guidance, a practice is customary "if it is recognisable as the norm and if failure to observe it is exceptional." For the factors to be considered in determining whether provision of living accommodation is customary see *Vertigan v Brady*.

HMRC accept (in their guidance at EIM 11351) that the following employees meet both the "better performance of the duties" and the "customary" tests:

- police officers;
- Ministry of Defence police;
- prison governors, officers and chaplains;
- clergymen and ministers of religion unless engaged on purely administrative duties;
- members of HM Forces;
- members of the Diplomatic Service;
- managers of newsagent shops that have paper rounds, but not those that do not;
- managers of public houses living on the premises;
- managers of traditional off-licence shops, that is those with opening hours broadly equivalent to those of a public house, but not those only open from 9am until 5pm or similar;
- in boarding schools (including schools where some of the pupils are boarders) where staff are provided with accommodation on or near the school premises:
  - head teacher,
  - other teachers with pastoral or other irregular contractual responsibilities outside normal school hours (for example house masters),
  - bursar,
  - matron, nurse and doctor.
- stable staff of racehorse trainers who live on the premises and certain key workers who live close to the stables.

Veterinary surgeons assisting in veterinary practices, and managers of camping and caravan sites living on or adjacent to the site, are accepted as meeting the "customary" test but the question of whether or not the "better performance of the duties" test is met is considered by HMRC on a case by case basis (see EIM 11352).

Security threat

The conditions required for this test to apply are a high hurdle to overcome. The sort of person who may qualify for this relief is an employee under a genuine terrorist threat to his or her life. HMRC emphasise that a security threat must be to the well-being of the employee and not to his or her property and therefore the exemption is not granted when living accommodation is given to an employee to provide security against attacks against his employer's stock or premises.

Law: TCGA 1992, s. 222(8A)(a)
Case: *Vertigan v Brady* [1988] STC 91
Guidance: EIM 11361, 11362

5.2.3   The self-employed

An individual is also occupying job-related accommodation if he has entered into an arm's length contract which requires him (or his spouse or civil partner) to carry on a trade, profession or vocation on another person's premises (or land) and to live on those premises or other premises supplied by that person.

The exemption for self-employed individuals will not apply if the living accommodation is in whole or part provided by either a company in which the person[1] (or his spouse or civil partner) has a material interest (see **5.2.4** below) or by a person(s) with whom the person carries on a trade or partnership.

---

[1] Section 222(8C) uses the term "borrower". It is suggested that is a drafting oversight which resulted from the insertion of the stand-alone definition of "job-related accommodation" which appeared in ICTA 1988, s. 356 for the purposes of mortgage interest relief but which was abolished in 1999. FA 1999, s. 38 and Sch. 4 inserted consequential amendments to TCGA 1992, s. 222 to include the same definition of job-related accommodation for the purposes of CGT and main residence relief but failed to change the old wording from "borrower" to "person" or "individual".

Examples of self-employed individuals who are likely to qualify for this extension of relief may be those who participate in and run franchise enterprises (for instance a takeaway restaurant or fast food outlet with late opening hours) and owners/managers of public houses who have a lease or under-lease with a brewery.

Law: TCGA 1992, s. 222(8A)(b)

5.2.4 Company directors

If the living accommodation is provided by a company to an employee who is a director of that company or any associated company[2], the extension of relief can only apply if the following conditions are met.

The first condition is that the director must not have a material interest in the company. This term has the same meaning here as in ITEPA 2003, s. 68. In summary, a person has a material interest if:

- he, or any of his associates, is the beneficial owner of, or is able to control, more than 5% of the ordinary share capital of the company; or

- if the company is a close company, he or any of his associates is entitled to acquire more than 5% of the assets potentially available for distribution among participators.

The second condition is that one of the following applies:

- the director is a full-time working director, i.e. one who is required to devote substantially the whole of his time to the service of the company in a managerial or technical capacity;

- the company is non-profit making, meaning that it does not carry on a trade and its functions do not consist wholly or mainly in the holding of investments or other property; or

- the company is a charitable company.

Law: TCGA 1992, s. 222 (8C), (8D); ITEPA 2003, s. 67(3)
Guidance: EIM 11342, 11347, 11351, 11352

---

[2] TCGA 1992, s. 222(8D)(a): a company is an "associated company" of another if one of them has control of the other or both are under the control of the same person.

5.3 Intention to occupy the property

The extended relief for job-related accommodation applies only if the individual in question "intends in due course to occupy the dwelling-house or part of a dwelling-house as his only or main residence".

There are two conflicting analyses[3] in relation to this requirement.

The first view warns in favour of a protective election as there is nothing in the legislation which prescribes how an intention to occupy a dwelling may be established. It is suggested that it would be prudent to assume that if in fact the dwelling was let out for a prolonged period after the job-related accommodation ceased to be provided, or if the dwelling was never occupied (because it was ultimately sold), a claim that a genuine intention to occupy ever existed would be seriously jeopardised.

The second view interprets the "intention" condition in a broader sense and concludes that it is not necessary to occupy the alternative dwelling-house once the job-related accommodation ceases to be available as long as the intention to occupy remains throughout. It is suggested that an individual could have a series of own dwelling-houses provided that the intention to occupy them eventually as a residence is maintained.

HMRC's guidance at CG 64555 seems to confirm the second and more generous analysis of the requirement of an intention to occupy the dwelling as a main residence. The guidance explains that even in cases where an individual "never actually occupies the dwelling-house that they intended to occupy due to a change in circumstances or some other reason" relief would still be available in full as long as the individual consistently intended to occupy it.

In the author's view, an intention is likely to be validated by cogent evidence supporting it and taxpayers should be advised to keep sufficient records of their plans and intentions to move from job-related accommodation to their own property. A claim for relief on

---

[3] Deduced from commentary in the professional press.

this basis should be made when the taxpayer is robust about his intentions and is willing (potentially) to be cross-examined about it in a Tribunal.

Law: TCGA 1992, s. 222(8)(b)

Guidance: CG 64555

5.4　Interaction with elections

As discussed above, s. 222(8) treats a dwelling-house as a residence if it is owned but is unoccupied because job-related accommodation is provided instead. However, this provision does not deem that "residence" to be an only or main residence for the purpose of main residence relief. For this reason, it will be necessary (and indeed would amount to good tax planning) to nominate which dwelling-house should be treated as the main residence for a particular period of time. The nomination should put matters beyond doubt and does not necessarily have to reflect the reality of the situation; in other words, an individual may elect whichever residence he prefers.

Guidance: CG 64485

5.5　Letting or use of dwelling-house is irrelevant

There is no provision in the legislation that prevents an individual who is occupying job-related living accommodation, and who has correctly elected for his own property to be treated as his main residence, from letting out his dwelling or using it for some other purpose. However, it is important to note and to be alert to cases where the lease of the dwelling-house extends beyond the period of expected occupation of the job-related accommodation, as this would be likely to amount to evidence that there was no real intention to occupy the dwelling-house at the end of the period.

Guidance: CG 64555

5.6　Interaction with allowable absences

As discussed above, in a case where an individual is provided with job-related living accommodation, and that individual holds an interest in another dwelling which fulfils the "intention to occupy" test, then that dwelling is treated as a residence. Two possible options may follow:

1. if there is just one dwelling-house in which the individual holds an interest (within the meaning of s. 222), then that dwelling will be treated as the only residence; or

2. if there is more than one residence owned or leased by the individual, one residence of his choice may become the elected main residence (see **8.3** below).

As one dwelling-house is treated as the main residence for the purpose of the relief, absences will also be permitted provided that both *before* and *after* each absence, there was a time when the dwelling-house was the individual's main residence by virtue of the job-related living accommodation provisions (s. 222(8)). Because s. 222(8) is a deeming provision and no actual occupation is required, it is inconsequential if, on return from a permitted absence, the individual occupies living accommodation provided by a different employer or under a different contract.

Example

Julian is a green keeper at Yield Golf Club in Kent who is required to live on site as the club has a history of burglaries and turf theft.

Julian owns a cottage inherited from his great-uncle in Dorset which he intends to move into upon his retirement. The cottage is used in the summers for furnished holiday lets.

In January 2014 (during low golfing season), Julian is offered an opportunity to work at an associated club in La Manga and decides to let out his cottage in Dorset on a short-hold tenancy and he moves to Spain for six years.

Upon his return, his position as green keeper at Yield has naturally been taken by another person but he manages to find a job at another golf club in Essex which also provides living accommodation.

The six years' absence working outside the UK are allowable under s. 223(3)(b) and the before and after requirement in s. 223(3A) and (3B) is fulfilled by the provision of the job-related accommodation back in the UK, albeit by different employers. The Dorset cottage is therefore likely to be eligible for full main residence relief for the duration of Julian's work abroad. It would, however, be prudent to make a main residence election in favour of the cottage.

5.7 Relief on employment relocation and home purchase agreements

Main residence relief is also extended to the disposal of residences under certain agreements with an employer. These provisions are contained in TCGA 1992, s. 225C which came into being by enactment of former Extra-Statutory Concession D37 with effect from 6 April 2009.

Section 225C applies where:

(a)   an individual disposes of, or an interest in, his only or main residence;

(b)   the individual has to dispose of his main residence as a consequence of relocation of his employment as required by the individual's employer or that of a co-owner[4] of the residence; and

(c)   the disposal of the residence is pursuant to a home purchase agreement.

A "home purchase agreement" is defined as an agreement made with the employer, or a person operating under an agreement with the employer (described as "the purchaser"), under which the individual is entitled to receive a share of any profit made by the purchaser on a subsequent sale of the same residence.

Under normal CGT rules a "right" to receive a profit share from a future disposal is treated as a disposal falling within TCGA 1992, s. 22 (a capital sum deriving from an asset). As such, the effect of the exemption is for any profit share to be treated as a gain attributable to the original disposal of the individual's main residence but which accrues at the time any profit sum is received (TCGA 1992, s. 225C(2)). There is, however, a three year time limit from the date of the initial disposal of the residence for any sums to be received.

The use of the words "required by the employer" in s. 225C(1)(b) point to this exemption being available only to those who have an

---

[4] This is defined by s. 225C(3)(b) as another individual who holds an interest in the dwelling-house (or part) jointly or in common with any individual, whether or not the interests of the co-owners are equal. This includes, but is not limited to, spouses and civil partners.

employment relationship, i.e. employees or office holders (e.g. directors).

Former ESC D37 restricted exemption to situations where the employer set up "arm's length" relocation arrangements for his employees, usually with a relocation agency. However s. 225C extended the exemption by including any arrangements made directly with the employer within the definition of "home purchase agreement".

Law: TCGA 1992, s. 22; 225C; *Extra-Statutory Concessions Order* 2009/730 art. 10(1)
Concession: Former ESC D37

6. Main or only residence relief in practice

6.1 Income tax versus CGT

Even before the gain made on a disposal of a dwelling-house and land may be treated as qualifying for main residence relief, the owner (or his adviser) must first consider whether an income tax charge may arise on gains from transactions in land. Income tax takes priority over capital gains tax (this is unsurprising since the rates of income tax are significantly higher than the rates of CGT and the income tax personal allowance is likely to be fully used up by other employment or trading income).

HMRC therefore explain to their officers (at CG 65200) that:

> "Before applying TCGA92/S224 (3) you should always consider the possibility that the taxpayer has undertaken an adventure in the nature of trade."

The likelihood of a finding of "a venture in the nature of a trade" in relation to the disposal of a dwelling-house is beyond the scope of this work. However, in cases where the landowner has a history of purchasing, renovating and selling properties at a profit, especially if the taxpayer happens to be in the building trade, an assessment to income tax may be increasingly difficult to resist. For a case which deals with this precise issue see *Kirky v Hughes*.

In practice, in a case where HMRC doubt the validity of main residence relief for a transaction, it is not uncommon for taxpayers to receive assessments to both income tax and capital gains tax in the alternative. If both income tax and CGT are not assessed in the alternative, there is a real risk that HMRC may lose out on tax in the event of a successful appeal.

The author was involved in an unreported case where HMRC raised a closure notice and a discovery assessment assessing a taxpayer to income tax for two tax years on the grounds that he had been trading as a property developer and that a series of three sales of houses (in a four-year period) amounted to a trade. In that case (possibly due to an oversight) no assessments to CGT had been raised and, when HMRC belatedly tried to amend their closure notice and discovery assessment, they were barred from doing so by the First-tier Tribunal. This was on the basis that HMRC had "nailed their colours firmly to the mast" on the issue of trading throughout their dealings with the taxpayer and that it would be unfair to the taxpayer to introduce the CGT issue in relation to his appeal against the assessments.

Case: *Kirkby v Hughes (HMIT)* (1992) 65 TC 532
Guidance: CG 65200

6.2 Scheme of the relief

HMRC's *Capital Gains Manual* at CG 64200 describes the scheme of main residence relief as follows:

> "The purpose of the relief is to enable a person to replace their existing home with another home of similar value by ensuring that the proceeds of sale of the old home are not diminished by a charge to Capital Gains Tax. So in most cases the gain arising on the disposal of a person's home is relieved from Capital Gains Tax."

The guidance moves on to outline the operation of the relief by highlighting twelve key areas:

- identification of the dwelling-house (see **3.1-3.4** above);
- identification of an individual's only or main residence (see **Chapter 2**);
- part of a dwelling-house used as an individual's only or main residence (see **3.5** above);
- the period for which entitlement to relief is considered (see **6.5** below);
- identification of the garden or grounds of the residence (see **4.1-4.3** above);
- determination of the permitted area of garden or grounds (see **4.4-4.5** above);
- computation of relief (see **6.4*ff.*** below);
- exchanges of interests in residences (see **3.8** above);
- acquisition of or expenditure on the residence for the purpose of realising a gain (see **9.4** below);

- division of the residence on separation or divorce or dissolution of a civil partnership (see **10.2** below);
- private residence relief on disposal of settled property (see **11.1** below);
- residence provided for a dependent relative (see **Chapter 12**).

For practical purposes this book will deal with each topic (though not in the order specified in the manual), highlighting areas where the guidance may be at odds with the legislation and with the Courts' interpretation of the various provisions.

Law: TCGA 1992, s. 222(1)
Guidance: CG 64200

6.3 How the relief works in practice

As a general rule, main residence relief is automatic (except where trusts and personal representatives are concerned – see **Chapter 11** below); there is no need to make a claim for the relief to apply or even disclose a fully exempt gain on a tax return.

There are exceptions to the general rule. For instance, if a dwelling-house has been sold and its garden or grounds exceeded the permitted area of 0.5 ha (even if the entire area of land was occupied for the reasonable enjoyment of the house at the time of disposal), the disposal and proceeds of sale, as well as the exact permitted area, will need to be disclosed on a tax return.

6.4 Amount and computation of relief

The quantum of any relief due will depend on the length of time during the period of ownership that the dwelling-house and gardens were occupied as the only or main residence of the person making the disposal (except for the last 18 months of the period of ownership for disposals after 5 April 2014 or 36 months[1] for those before; see **6.6.1** below) (TCGA 1992, s. 223(1)).

The sale proceeds (and expenditure) will have to be apportioned depending on the period of ownership and any absences from the

---

[1] In fact, the "final" period of ownership was in the past even shorter – 12 months – for disposals before 6 April 1980, and it was 24 months for disposals between 6 April 1980 and 18 March 1991.

property. The apportionment fraction will consist of the length of the part or parts of the period of ownership during which the dwelling-house (or part of it) was occupied as the person's main or only residence, including the last 18 months of deemed occupation, divided by the length of the period of occupation, as follows:

$$\text{Gain x } \frac{\text{Period of occupation as main residence}^2}{\text{Period of ownership}}$$

Section 223 does not prescribe how the periods are to be measured and so a common sense approach should be applied. A reasonable approach would be for shorter periods to be counted in days and for longer periods to be measured in months.

Period of ownership

Although the term "period of ownership" is a key component in the computation of main residence relief, there is no statutory definition of the term and there are no helpful hints as to when this period should be deemed to start. In stark contrast with provisions dealing with stamp duty land tax, TCGA 1992, s. 222 does not distinguish between entering into a contract to purchase a dwelling-house, substantial performance of that contract or legal completion. In the circumstances, and using a common sense approach, the term should be given its natural and ordinary meaning.

In the author's view, the period of ownership of a residence starts when the persons acquiring the interest in the dwelling-house become legally entitled to occupy it (right to physical possession). If, contrary to this view, the period of ownership starts when contracts are exchanged it would bring about situations when (for reasons outside of the owners' control) there is a long gap before the owners can start living in their home but for which they would be liable to CGT. This would be an undesirable consequence taking into account the stated policy behind the relief (to exempt from CGT liability any gain made on the disposal of a person's home in light of the "evil of inflation" – *Sansom v Peay*).

In *Higgins*, the FTT had to consider whether or not the taxpayer was entitled to main residence relief on a disposal of a flat that had been purchased off-plan six years earlier. Mr Higgins paid a deposit of

---

2 Including the last 18 months.

£5,000 in 2004 and in 2006 entered into a contract for the lease of an apartment that would be built by a developer. There were delays occasioned by the financial crisis of 2008 and the work on the building block only began in late 2009. Under the terms of the contract, legal completion had to take place by 30 June 2012 or Mr Higgins would have a right to rescind the contract.

The taxpayer had no right to occupy the apartment until 5 January 2010 when legal completion took effect. From that date onwards, Mr Higgins occupied the apartment as his main residence until the date of disposal in January 2012.

In terms of residential arrangements, Mr Higgins sold his previously occupied residence in July 2007 and in the interim period lived with his parents, travelled and stayed in another buy-to-let property owned by him that had become available.

The FTT held that the taxpayer was entitled to full main residence relief for the entire period of ownership notwithstanding the long period when Mr Higgins could not physically occupy the property. The Tribunal agreed with the author's view that the term "period of ownership" should be given its natural and ordinary meaning. Using a purposive construction, a taxpayer who occupies a residence as soon as he or she is able (legally and physically) to do so, should be entitled to the relief. The FTT rejected HMRC's argument that TCGA 1992, s. 28 applied to determine the period of ownership for all purposes because the wording of s. 222(7) referred to the "first acquisition" of multiple interests in a property as the time when the period of ownership begins. According to the FTT, the existence of ESC D49 supported their view and sought to prevent "absurd and perverse results".

It should be noted that this case is one of two HMRC's appeals against an unfavourable main residence decision in the FTT; the Upper Tribunal is expected to hear a full appeal in June 2018.

Law: TCGA 1992, s. 28, 222(7), 223

Cases: *Sansom & Another (Ridge Settlement Trustees) v Peay (HMIT)* [1976] 1 WLR 1073, (1976) 52 TC 1; *Higgins v HMRC* [2017] UKFTT 236 (TC)

Guidance: ESC D49

Periods of ownership versus period of occupation before 31 March 1982

According to TCGA 1992, s. 223(7), any periods of ownership before 31 March 1982 are usually ignored when computing the amount of relief (unless the only period of occupation as a main residence was before this date in which case relief is still given for the last 18 months of ownership). This restriction should not be confused with the entitlement to main residence relief pursuant to s. 222 which provides for a property to be considered as an individual's main or only residence if the dwelling-house has been occupied as a residence at *any* time during the period of ownership (even if before 1982). When entering periods of occupation and ownership into the formula above (at **5.4**) only periods from 31 March 1982 should be taken into account.

Example

Mari inherited a flat in 1978 and occupied it as her main residence until 1981 when she moved to a larger house with her boyfriend and future husband. Mari kept her flat as an occasional study and storage space for the first five years and let it out for the rest. She finally sold it in order to buy a holiday home abroad on 30 June 2014. In calculating the periods of ownership and occupation, only years from 31 March 1982 are counted. So, the total period of (deemed) occupation is 1.5 years (last 18 months of ownership) over a total of 32.25 years of ownership. As she did not occupy the flat again after her departure in 1981 no other periods of allowable absences will apply.

Law: TCGA 1992, s. 223(2), (7)

Allowable losses?

In the unlikely event that a dwelling-house is sold for less than its original base cost, i.e. it is sold at a loss, the loss will not count as an allowable loss to the extent that the gain would have been exempt or not a "chargeable gain" – TCGA 1992, s. 16(2).

There are three exceptions to this rule:

1. If lettings relief (see **7.3** below) is due. This is because TCGA 1992, s. 223(4) restricts the gain made during a period the dwelling-house was let out to a third party by

three limits (the lowest of the amount of chargeable gain arising as a result of the letting, the amount of main residence relief due, or £40,000) but these limits cannot be applied if no gain arises. There is no further restriction of the allowable loss in such cases (see also CG 65080).

2. Where the dwelling-house is occupied under the terms of a settlement (see **11.2** below). The trustees may make a claim for main residence relief under s. 225 for disposals after 10 December 2003. If a loss is made on a disposal there will be no scope for a claim pursuant to s. 225 and therefore any losses will be allowable (see also CG 65080).

3. Where a dwelling-house is provided for a dependent relative (see **12.1** below). Again a claim by an individual may be made for main residence relief under s. 226 but if no claim is made then s. 226 will not apply. Any losses made may be restricted by any periods of occupation of the dwelling-house as the individual's main or only residence but will not be affected by the occupation of a dependent relative (see also CG 65080).

Law: TCGA 1992, s. 16(2); s. 223(1), (2)
Guidance: CG 65080

6.5 Periods of deemed occupation as main residence

In what is considered a reasonable and generous approach in the legislation, TCGA 1992, s. 223 provides for certain periods of absence from a residence to be deemed as actual occupation for the purposes of calculating main residence relief. In most cases, of course, the individual or individuals disposing of a dwelling-house would have owned it and occupied it as a residence for the entire period of ownership and the full gain will be relieved. In the remainder of cases, there may be extended periods when the owner is absent from the residence either deliberately or for reasons outside his control; it is in these cases that the intricacies of the rules on main residence relief will need to be considered carefully and, if possible, included in any tax planning before a decision to leave the property is made.

"Period of absence" is defined in s. 223(7) as a period during which the dwelling-house or part of the dwelling-house was not the individual's only or main residence and throughout which he had no residence or main residence eligible for [main residence] relief. A strict interpretation of s. 223(7) means that the extensions of relief provided by s. 223 will not be available when there is a second residence which could benefit from main residence relief. In practice, an election in favour of the residence from which the individual is absent is sufficient to satisfy HMRC that there was "no residence or main residence *eligible*" for main residence relief.

Law: TCGA 1992, s. 223(7)

6.6   Allowable absences

6.6.1   The last 18 months of the period of ownership – general rule

TCGA 1992, s. 223(1) provides:

> "No part of a gain to which section 222 applies shall be a chargeable gain if the dwelling-house or part of the dwelling-house has been the individual's only or main residence throughout the period of ownership, **or throughout the period of ownership except for all or any part of the last 18 months of that period.**"

This means in practice that even if one is occupying another dwelling-house as a main residence but elects for the original residence to be the main residence for these purposes, the last 18 months of the ownership period will be fully exempt from CGT, and this could represent a fair saving for the individual owner. The saving used to be far more generous prior to the introduction of FA 2014, s. 58(2)(a) which halved the "final" exempt period from 36 months to 18 months. The change covers gains accruing on or after 6 April 2014.

HMRC's guidance explains at CG 64985 that "the purpose of the final period exemption is to help the owner occupier who puts his or her house up for sale but cannot find a buyer". Nevertheless, HMRC accept that the exemption always applies, whatever the reasons or occupation of the dwelling-house during this period.

6.6.2 The last 36 months – disabled owners or those in care homes

The changes in FA 2014, considered immediately above, provide an exception to the halved final period of ownership for disabled people and people in care homes. In certain circumstances the time is extended to the previous 36 months if one of the two sets of conditions is met, as below.

Law: TCGA 1992, s. 225E(1), (4)

Set 1 (individual is disabled)

At the time of the disposal:

    a. the individual is a disabled person or a long-term resident in a care home; and

    b. he or she does not have any other relevant right in relation to a private residence.

"Disabled person" is defined in FA 2005, Sch. 1A, para. 1 as a person who has a mental health disorder which renders him incapable of administering his property or managing his own affairs or is in receipt of one of the following:

- attendance allowance;
- disability allowance;
- personal independence payment;
- increased disablement pension;
- constant attendance allowance; or
- armed forces independence payment.

A "long-term resident" in a care home is defined as a person who is resident in such a home and has been there (or can reasonably be expected to be resident there) for at least three months.

Law: TCGA 1992, s. 225E(2), (5)

Set 2 (spouse is disabled)

At the time of the disposal:

    (a) the individual's spouse or civil partner is a disabled person or a long-term resident in a care home; and

(b)   neither the individual nor the individual's spouse or civil partner has any other relevant right in relation to a private residence.

A person is deemed to have "any other relevant right in relation to a private residence" at the time of the disposal if two conditions are met. The first condition is that either:

(a)   that person owns or holds an interest in a dwelling-house (or part thereof) which was not the dwelling-house in relation to which a gain accrued; or

(b)   the person is entitled to occupy the dwelling-house (or part thereof) under the terms of a settlement and the trustees own or hold an interest in a dwelling-house (or part thereof) which is not the dwelling-house in relation to which a gain accrued;

The second condition is that TCGA 1992, s. 222 would have applied to any gain accruing on the disposal of that other residence or would have done if an election (pursuant to TCGA 1992, s. 222(5)) had been made.

Law: TCGA 1992, s. 225E(3), (6)

Further observations

Two things may be said about these relatively new provisions.

The first is that the exception does not cover or apply to unmarried couples even if one of the partners is disabled and all the conditions are satisfied.

The second is that the mere existence of a second home which is occupied as a residence will prevent the extension of time even if this dwelling has deliberately never been elected as a main residence so that the relief would have never applied to it. This result seems unfair and is perhaps unintended. It is suggested that this unfair result could be alleviated by simply making an election in favour of the main residence which deliberately excludes the second home from the scope of s. 222. In a case where an election notice has been made in favour of the main dwelling-house which will be disposed of (as a consequence of or subsequent to the individual becoming disabled or taken into care), s. 222 would therefore not apply to any gain made on the disposal of the second dwelling-

111

house. In terms of the reference to "or would have applied if notice had been given" in TCGA 1992, s. 225E(6)(b), if notice has been given positively in favour of the main residence then s. 222 could not and would not apply to the disposal of the second residence.

The effect of s. 225E(6) is better illustrated by way of an example:

Example

Becky owns a third-floor purpose built flat in central London with no lift (where she stays from Monday to Friday) and a large country house that she inherited from her grandmother. After a completely unexpected brain haemorrhage, Becky loses motor functions on the left side of her body. As a result of her physical disability she has to be admitted into a care home for two and a half years whilst she recovers. Becky is advised that she will no longer be able to live in her flat as her mobility will be restricted even after therapy and she therefore decides to sell the flat before leaving the care home. She would appreciate and benefit from the country air and will move to her country house to continue her physiotherapy.

The new rules would have different effects on this scenario depending on whether or not Becky makes an election in favour of her main residence (being her London flat) before its disposal.

If Becky gives notice of an election, although she would own a second residence at the time of the disposal, s. 222 would not and could not apply to any gain made on that second residence because the election would preclude main residence relief. The words "or would have applied if notice had been given" become meaningless as an actual notice of election would exist in favour of the London flat only. Becky would therefore benefit from the extended final 36 months of ownership in computing her entitlement to the relief.

If Becky gives no notice of election and sells her main residence in London, the second country residence would fall foul of the condition in s. 225E(6)(b) as main residence relief would have (in theory) applied to any gain accruing on it or could have applied if an election had been made in its favour. The new 18-month final period of ownership would therefore apply.

Law: TCGA 1992, s. 222(5); 223(1), (7); 225E; FA 2005, Sch. 1A, para. 1; FA 2014, s. 58(2)(a)
Guidance: CG 64985

6.6.3   *Other periods – statutory overview*

In addition to the last 18 months of the period of ownership in TCGA 1992, s. 223(1), s. 223 sets out four periods of absence which for the purposes of main residence relief are treated as if there was actual occupation as an individual's only or main residence as follows:

"(3) For the purposes of subsections (1) and (2) above—

(a)   a period of absence not exceeding 3 years (or periods of absence which together did not exceed 3 years), and in addition

(b)   any period of absence throughout which the individual worked in an employment or office all the duties of which were performed outside the United Kingdom or lived with a spouse or civil partner who worked in such an employment or office, and in addition

(c)   any period of absence not exceeding 4 years (or periods of absence which together did not exceed 4 years) throughout which the individual was prevented from residing in the dwelling-house or part of the dwelling-house in consequence of the situation of his place of work or in consequence of any condition imposed by his employer requiring him to reside elsewhere, being a condition reasonably imposed to secure the effective performance by the employee of his duties, and in addition,

(d)   any period of absence not exceeding 4 years (or periods of absence which together did not exceed 4 years) throughout which the individual lived with a spouse or civil partner in respect of whom paragraph (c) applied in respect of that period (or periods),

shall be treated as if in that period of absence the dwelling-house or the part of the dwelling-house was the individual's only or main residence [if conditions A and B are met].

(3A) Condition A is that before the period there was a time when the dwelling-house was the individual's only or main residence.

(3B) Condition B is that after the period—

    (a)   in a case falling within paragraph (a), (b), (c) or (d) of subsection (3), there was a time when the dwelling-house was the individual's only or main residence,

    (b)   in a case falling within paragraph (b), (c) or (d) of that subsection, the individual was prevented from resuming residence in the dwelling-house in consequence of the situation of the individual's place of work or a condition imposed by the terms of the individual's employment requiring the individual to reside elsewhere, being a condition reasonably imposed to secure the effective performance by the employee of his duties, or

    (c)   in a case falling within paragraph (b), (c) or (d) of that subsection, the individual lived with a spouse or civil partner to whom paragraph (b) of this subsection applied."

6.6.4   *Any periods of up to three years*

According to s. 223(3)(a), any cumulative periods of absence for any reason whatsoever (including letting) amounting to a total of 36 months will be deemed to be periods of occupation by the individual seeking relief as long as the dwelling-house was occupied at some point during the ownership period as the individual's only or main residence *before* and *after* the absence (not necessarily immediately). A helpful way of illustrating these rules is to imagine a sandwich composed by a period of absence in the middle wedged between two periods of actual occupation either side. The legislation does not specify how long the periods of residence either side of an absence must be; it is likely to be a question of fact and degree depending on the circumstances of each case. An analysis of the quality of the occupation (rather than quantity), as well as the intentions of the individual, is likely to be paramount in determining whether any periods of occupation amounted to occupation as a residence.

This deemed period of occupation or allowable absence should not be confused with the final period of ownership (18 or 36 months: see **6.6.1** or **6.6.2** above). In order to benefit from the allowable absence(s) in s. 223(3)(a) there must be *actual* occupation of the dwelling-house as a residence after the period of absence; this means that the final period of ownership rule in s. 223(1) cannot be used to plug any gaps in the required occupation.

There is a slight question mark about aggregate periods which *exceed* three years in total. On a literal reading of s. 223(3)(a), it could be interpreted as an all or nothing provision, that is, any periods of longer than 36 months (regardless of the length of time) will fall outside the relief. HMRC's guidance at CG 65066 suggests that this is not how they interpret this part of the legislation and the lack of relevant case law indicates that this point has not been taken in practice.

6.6.5 *Unlimited periods of employment or office outside the UK*

Section 223(3)(b) provides that any absences dictated by the individual's employment or office outside of the United Kingdom will be treated as actual occupation of the dwelling-house as a residence. This extension of relief is dependent upon two conditions:

- first, all of the duties of the employment or office must be performed overseas during the entire period of absence; and

- second, no other residence must be eligible for main residence relief.

The strict consequence of s. 223(3)(b) is therefore that short periods of holiday spent in the UK are likely to be ignored but employment duties – however minimal – which are performed in the UK would cause the relief to fail. The words "throughout" and "all the duties" are support for this interpretation. HMRC's guidance also confirms this view (at CG 65040).

This interpretation of the provision appears to be in direct contradiction of the Parliamentary debates recorded when the predecessor to s. 223(3)(b) (FA 1965, s. 29(4)(b)) was introduced. The then Financial Secretary to the Treasury, Mr. Niall MacDermot, explained to the House of Commons:

> "With regard to the case of the man who goes overseas [to work full time] we are advised that the terms of the new subsection (4)(b) are wide enough to cover any period during which such an individual may visit this country either on leave or for purposes incidental to his employment, and he will still be entitled to the benefit of the exemption, even though during those periods he does not occupy the house which he owns."

The restrictive interpretation is also at odds with the statutory residence test (contained in FA 2013, Sch. 45, para. 14) and in particular the third automatic overseas test which specifically allows for a *de minimis* number of days spent in the UK and for incidental work to be carried out during those days[3].

In practice, due to changes introduced by FA 2015 (see **2.5** above) individuals who leave the UK for full-time work abroad and who during their period of non-residence dispose of their UK residence may now need to rely on the periods of deemed occupation in s. 223(3) in order to become fully eligible for main residence relief.

The obvious pitfall which could be encountered by an expatriate worker in such a situation would be a complete reliance on the reasonable terms of the statutory residence test (i.e. performing a small number of duties of the employment in the UK during his absence) whilst being blissfully unaware of the conflicting and far more restrictive rules in s. 223(3)(b).

The Chartered Institute of Taxation made submissions on this discrepancy and "the particular concern that the [non-UK resident capital gains] charge acts punitively on expatriates leaving the UK to work full-time abroad" both at the FB 2015 Consultation stage in late 2014 and following the introduction of the FA 2015 changes in April 2015 (see http://tinyurl.com/nzbn69n (a shortened link)).

---

[3] Para. 14(1)(c) provides that the number of days in a relevant tax year on which an individual does more than three hours' work in the UK must be less than 31.

The Institute urged HMRC to consider amending TCGA 1992, s. 223(3)(b) to bring it in line with Parliament's original intention and the statutory residence test (third automatic overseas test) but unfortunately no proposed amendments were drafted into the *Finance Bill* 2015-16 which was introduced to the House of Commons on 15 July 2015.

Finally, s. 223(3)(b) specifically refers to "employment" or "office" and effectively excludes those who are self-employed carrying on a trade, profession or vocation and those who work in the voluntary sector but who may not meet the three basic conditions of a contract of employment[4].

Law: TCGA 1992, s. 223(3)(b); FA 2015, s. 39 and Sch. 9; FB 2015-16
Guidance: CG 65040
Hansard debates: *Finance (No. 2) Bill* 1965: 2R, [712] 47, 64

Inability to resume residence after period of absence because of employment

The need to occupy the dwelling-house as a residence before and after the absence period will also apply to this extension of relief unless the individual was prevented from resuming residence in that dwelling-house by reason of the location of the individual's place of work or a term in his or her contract of employment which requires him or her to work and reside elsewhere (TCGA 1992, s. 223(3B)(b)). This legislative exception is relatively new and originated from Extra-Statutory Concession D4 which existed in relation to disposals made before 6 April 2009 (and which was enacted by the *Extra-Statutory Concessions Order* 2009/730 art. 8(3)).

ESC D4 provided (in very similar terms to s. 223(3B)(b)) that if after a period of absence abroad due to employment or office an individual was unable to resume residence in his (or her) previous home because the terms of his employment required him to work elsewhere, the period of absence would still satisfy the conditions in

---

[4] First, an obligation by the employee to provide work personally; second, mutuality of obligation and third, that the employee both expressly and impliedly agreed that he was subject to the employer's control sufficient to render the employer master.

117

223(3)(b) (absence on duties overseas) or (c) (other absences due to conditions of employment).

Spouses and civil partners

If the condition in s. 223(3)(b) is satisfied by one spouse or civil partner working in an employment or office abroad, it is also regarded as being satisfied by the other cohabiting spouse or civil partner. This provision originated from Extra-Statutory Concession D3 which was enacted by the *Extra-Statutory Concessions Order* 2009/730 art. 7(2) with effect for disposals made after 6 April 2009.

Law: TCGA 1992, s. 223(3)(b),(c), (3B)(b)
Concessions: ESC D3, D4

6.6.6   Up to four years due to the location of place of work

The last statutory allowable absence is a period of four years maximum (or aggregate periods of no more than four years) occasioned by the individual's terms of employment or the location of his place of work. The use of the term "work" indicates that this extension of relief (in contrast with the unlimited extension for employment outside the UK) applies equally to employees and to those carrying on a trade, profession or vocation.

Section 223(3)(c) provides that the individual must have been "prevented from residing" in his main residence:

- as a consequence of a reasonable condition imposed by his employer compelling him to live elsewhere; or
- due to the location of the place of work (in the UK or abroad; for instance, a transfer to another branch or office of the same employer).

The word "prevented" rules out any choice the individual may have on the matter, so in cases where the individual prefers to live in certain accommodation (for example, because it happens to shorten commuting time or because it is within a certain school catchment area), this extension will not apply.

In similar terms to the extension for unlimited periods of employment or office outside the UK, in order for the 4-year absence to be available, the individual must not have another residence eligible for relief (an election or nomination in favour of the main residence would put the matter beyond doubt) and the dwelling-house must in fact be occupied as a residence by the individual before and after (but not necessarily immediately) the absence period. The requirement to resume residence after an absence due to employment is also relaxed by s. 223(3B)(b) (previously ESC D4).

Spouses and civil partners

Again, if the conditions set out in s. 223(3)(c) are met by one spouse or civil partner, s. 223(3)(d) treats an absence of up to 4 years during which the couple lived together as a period or periods of actual occupation of the main residence by *both* spouses or civil partners.

Law: TCA 1992, s. 223(3)(c), (d); s. 223(3B)(b)
Concession: ESC D4

6.6.7 Several periods of absence for different reasons – an example

At CG 65065, HMRC set out a very helpful example of how all of the allowable absences listed above may be applied together in a single scenario:

HMRC example

An individual bought a dwelling-house in Bournemouth in January 2003 and lived in it as his only residence. In October 2003 his employer required him to work in Glasgow. He lived there in a flat provided by the employer until October 2008. Then his employer transferred him to work in Cologne and also provided a flat there. He ended his employment in March 2010 and toured Europe until November 2010. Then he returned to his dwelling-house in Bournemouth and occupied it as his only residence until he sold it in January 2014.

The whole of the period of ownership qualifies for relief for the following reasons

- January 2003-October 2003 – Only or main residence
- October 2003-October 2007 – four years absence by reason of employment, TCGA92/S223 (3)(c)

- October 2007-October 2008 – one year of absence for any reason, TCGA92/S223 (3)(a)

- October 2008-March 2010 – period of absence due to employment outside the United Kingdom, Section 223(3)(b)

- March 2010-November 2010 – seven months absence for whatever reason, Section 223(3)(a)

- November 2010-January 2014 – only or main residence.

The period of absence legislation is applied in the way which is of most benefit to the taxpayer. For example, if the period from October 2003 – October 2007 had been treated as qualifying primarily under Section 223(3)(a) that would have used up the three year allowance and so no relief would have been available for the period between March and November 2010.

The periods of absence are cumulative. In this example, the total qualifying period is seven years and two months.

6.6.8   Short delay by owner-occupier in taking up residence – new buildings or repairs and alterations

In cases where there is a delay in occupying the newly acquired dwelling-house as a residence, HMRC introduced Extra-Statutory Concession D49 (on 18 October 1994). According to this concession, full main residence relief will be due to an individual who has disposed of a dwelling-house which he was prevented from occupying due to the construction or extensive repair and refurbishment of a dwelling which is then used as the same individual's residence.

The concession will apply where an individual:

- acquires land on which he has a new dwelling built which is then occupied as his only or main residence; or

- purchases an existing dwelling and before occupying it undertakes alterations or redecorations; or

- completes the necessary steps for disposing of his previous residence. This effectively means that the individual would obtain relief for two dwelling-houses for the same period of ownership.

The period of delay should be no longer than one year unless there are circumstances outside the individual's control. In exceptional circumstances, the period of delay allowed may be extended to a maximum of two years. The terms of ESC D49 make it unnecessary for an election to be made between two residences owned at the same time and do not require the individual to move into the new or renovated dwelling immediately after conclusion of the building works. In the author's view the concession should continue to apply as long as the individual occupies the dwelling-house as a residence within the one year period (or two years if there is good reason).

Example 1

Alison and Mark purchase a three-bedroom detached house in Croydon on 26 July 2013. The house was previously owned by an elderly couple who had to be taken into care. As a result of the couple's deteriorating health, the house had not been updated for decades and therefore Alison and Mark have to undertake extensive works of updating and renovation.

They start work the day after completion and essentially remove all of the interior decorations. They plan to introduce a new kitchen, bathroom, electrical and plumbing system as well as some minor structural work to the living room and a new shower room downstairs. They move in with Alison's parents in the interim and obtain exemption from Council Tax because their dwelling-house is uninhabitable.

They expect to be done with the work within 9 to 12 months but in May 2014 the builders discover subsidence. The subsidence had not been caught by their surveyor's report, the cost of repairing the damage is outside their budget and therefore they have to make a claim against the surveyor, which takes a further eight months. The house is finally made safe and completed on 25 March 2015 and Alison and Mark move in straight afterwards.

Since the issue of subsidence was outside the couple's control, and impossible for them to foresee, it is likely that HMRC would accept the total delay of 20 months as falling within the terms of ESC D49. If Alison and Mark had simply run out of funds, preventing them from completing the renovations, this reason may not have counted as an exceptional circumstance.

Example 2

Mr and Mrs Smith purchased three properties in Harrogate in the years 2002 and 2003. They wished to convert the three properties into a single dwelling-house and main residence. The chronology of the purchases was complex as follows:

Property	Date of Exchange	Date of Completion	a. Planning permission for change of use b. Building operations c. Move-in date
1	11 June 2002	12 July 2002	PP submitted in January 2003 Granted on 4 September 2003 and building works commenced. Moved in on 27 October 2005
2	11 June 2002	21 Sept 2002	Granted PP on 4 September 2003 Moved in on 24 November 2004
3	28 Mar 2003	17 April 2003	Moved in on 1 September 2004

Notes

1. The costs for the entire construction project were substantial, at approximately £5.5m. The family were unable to move into their new properties after purchase and remained in their previous residence during the construction works. The completion of the construction works on the development was broken down into phases with the family moving into each part as the properties were finished. The buildings were not occupied by anyone else during the construction works and they were for all intents and purposes uninhabitable. Property 1 was the last one to be fully occupied by the family in October 2005.

122

2. Mr and Mrs Smith occupied the building as a single dwelling-house and their only residence for nearly 10 years.

3. The house was eventually sold on 20 January 2015 for a substantial capital gain.

As there is no provision in the legislation for delays in occupation of a main residence by reason of refurbishment or renovation works, strictly speaking, the taxpayers would be entitled to main residence relief from the date they occupied each of the three properties (taking into account the value and enhancement expenditure for each dwelling) and not from date of completion. The recent case of *Higgins* suggests that the period of ownership commences when an individual becomes legally and physically entitled to occupy the dwelling in question (see **6.4** above).

It is suggested that in accordance with the terms of ESC D49, entitlement to main residence relief is not on an "all or nothing" basis. Notwithstanding this, the time that elapsed when applying and obtaining planning permission would be taken into account in considering any time extension. Having said that, HMRC are likely to grant relief in part on the gains accrued on some of the properties. Property 3 is likely to benefit from the concession and possibly Property 2 (although it was occupied two months outside the stated maximum)[5]. The Smiths are, however, unlikely to persuade HMRC to extend relief in respect of Property 1 because of the substantial delay in occupation of over three years.

ESC D49 does not apply to inherited property

Advisers and their clients should be aware that the terms of Extra-Statutory Concession D49 are unlikely to cover situations where the dwelling-house has been inherited by the owner-occupier. The wording of the ESC is very specific in that it refers to situations where an individual "*acquires* land" or "*purchases* an existing house". Inheriting a property does not fall within either of these descriptions (because a dwelling is not strictly "land" and because an inheritance is not a "purchase") and is therefore unlikely to benefit from the relaxation. In these cases, the legatee would have to

---

[5] In appropriate cases, HMRC have a wide discretion under their care and management powers to extend time limits or extra-statutory concessions: *R v Inland Revenue Commissioners, ex parte Unilever* [1996] STC 681.

move in and occupy the property as his or her main residence immediately after the date of death (which is when the period of ownership starts). In practice, an immediate move is very unlikely to happen and so the period between the date of death and actual occupation will be fully chargeable to CGT. HMRC's guidance does not refer to this point in relation to ESC D49 but explains the effect of the deemed ownership period at CG 64925.

Guidance: CG 64925; CG 65065
Concession: ESC D49

7.   Lettings relief

7.1   Overview

A further extension to the exemption from CGT on capital gains accrued on the disposal of an individual's only or main residence applies where the owner (who must, at some point during his ownership, have occupied the property as his only or main residence) lets the whole or part of his dwelling-house as residential accommodation. This extension is contained in s. 223(4) which provides:

223.   Amount of relief

(4)   **Where** a gain to which section 222 applies accrues to any individual and **the dwelling-house in question or any part of it** is or **has** at any time in his period of ownership **been wholly or partly let** by him **as residential accommodation, the part of the gain**, if any, which (apart from this subsection) would be a chargeable gain by reason of the letting, **shall be such a gain only to the extent**, if any, **to which it exceeds** whichever is **the lesser of—**

   (a)   the part of the gain which is not a chargeable gain by virtue of the provisions of subsection (1) to (3) above; and

   (b)   £40,000.

Lettings relief is not restricted to dwelling-houses owned in the UK. This means that a home owner could potentially elect for an overseas residence, which is used for some months of the year but let out as furnished holiday accommodation for the rest of the tax year, to be treated as his or her main residence and still benefit from lettings relief.

7.2   Residential lettings

The meaning for the purposes of this sub-section of "let as residential accommodation" was analysed by the Court of Appeal in the case of *Owen v Elliott*. In that case, the taxpayer and his wife owned a private hotel business in Eastbourne and would live during the summer months in a small annex attached to the main house, and at the end of the summer in the main house along with a very few remaining guests. The guests were fully catered for. After an eventual disposal of the entire property, it was agreed with the Revenue that one third of the realised gain would qualify for main residence relief and that the word "let" could include a licence to occupy. However, there was a dispute between the parties as to whether or not there was an entitlement to lettings relief; the Revenue's inspector disagreed that the property had been let to guests and thus had been "let by him as residential accommodation". Both the General Commissioners and the High Court on appeal held that "the taking in of boarders" did not amount to letting as residential accommodation because they did not *intend* to occupy the property as their home.

The Court of Appeal, Fox LJ (with whom the other judges agreed), held that although *Capital Gains Tax Act* 1979, s. 101 (now TCGA 1992, s. 222) was concerned with dwelling-houses that could reasonably be called "homes", there was nothing in s. 80(1) (now TCGA 1992, s. 223(4)) which corresponded to those provisions and:

> "nothing in its provisions to displace the admitted meaning of the words 'residential accommodation' as a matter of the ordinary use of the English language. If the draftsman of section 80 wanted to introduce a requirement of a home as a basis for the granting of the relief in respect of the relevant letting...it [is] impossible to believe that he would not have used language which made that plain."

It is not difficult to see why the Court of Appeal came to this decision in the above case. Applying common sense to the legislation, the Revenue's suggested test of "likely to be used as a home" was subjective and entirely dependent on the intentions of the occupant. The application of this test would have been extremely difficult to ascertain in individual cases and unworkable in practice.

HMRC's Guidance at CG 64713 adds that in order to benefit from the decision in *Owen v Elliott*, any letting should be conducted on a commercial basis, although not necessarily in exchange for money.

HMRC seem happy to accept genuine agreements to provide services (or money's worth) in exchange for accommodation.

Law: TCGA 1992, s. 222, s. 223(4)
Case: *Owen v Elliott (HMIT)* [1990] Ch 786, [1990] STC 469
Guidance: CG 64710*ff.*

7.3 Amount of lettings relief

7.3.1 General principle

In essence, the amount of lettings relief will be the *lowest* of three figures:

1. the gain arising by reason of the letting;
2. the amount of the only or main residence relief available; or
3. a fixed figure of £40,000.

The restriction to the amount of only or main residence relief available can be a decisive factor in considering an election or disposal of a residence and one of the most commonly missed constraints of s. 223. The restriction prevents house owners from eliminating (or significantly reducing) a capital gain by electing for a dwelling-house to be their main residence for a very short period during which the property is not let. (For a discussion on elections see **Chapter 8**).

The amount of lettings relief applies per individual and therefore in cases where the dwelling-house is jointly owned the total relief is calculated by reference to each owner. For the purposes of this relief, spouses and civil partners are treated as other joint owners[1] and therefore the maximum relief for a couple could be £80,000. The total relief should apply provided that the relevant letting occurred during the personal ownership period of each spouse or civil partner as there is no provision deeming the lettings by one spouse or civil partner to be lettings by the other.

In most cases lettings relief is a generous extension of main residence relief which may well wipe out all of the chargeable gain

---

[1] HMRC caveat this treatment by insisting on genuine joint ownership.

127

realised in relation to a main residence. It should be noted however that lettings relief cannot be used to turn that gain into a loss.

In practice, HMRC are likely to accept that any absence (for whatever reason) in which the property is let out will qualify for lettings relief under s. 223(4). On a strict reading of the legislation, the extension of relief is available exclusively in cases where there would otherwise be a chargeable gain but for the letting. It is also important to note that in order for lettings relief to be available and effective, and in contrast with allowable absences under s. 223(1) to (3B), there is no requirement for the individual to re-occupy the dwelling-house as his residence.

Finally, periods of actual and deemed occupation (allowable absences) take priority over lettings relief. For instance, if an individual owns a dwelling-house which he intends to occupy as his main residence but he is required to live in job-related accommodation (or that of his spouse or civil partner), and the house is let out during the entire period, there is no need to consider lettings relief as any gain is likely to be exempt under the provisions in s. 222(8) as long as the individual is able to show an intention to occupy the house eventually as a residence (see **Chapter 5** for the conditions for job-related accommodation relief).

Example

Nancy purchases a house on 1 August 2005 and occupies it as a home until 31 July 2010. Nancy moves in with her aunt who needs care for an entire year and leaves her house unoccupied. After this time Nancy decides to move to a smaller flat in order to save money for a long-term trip around the world and she lets her house to residential tenants on 1 August 2011. Nancy travels around the world for some time and when she returns to the UK she moves back in with her aunt (now recovered) until she sells her house on 1 August 2015. She realises a gain of £100,000 before any reliefs.

As a result of not re-occupying the house before its sale, Nancy will not be able to benefit from the allowable absence of "any periods of up to 3 years" (as provided in TCGA 1992, s. 223(3)(a), see **6.6.4** for commentary on this deemed period of occupation) but as she occupied it for five years as her only residence, she will be entitled to the last 18 months of her period of ownership (a total of six and a half years).

As such, the lettings relief available would be the lowest of:

1. The main residence relief: £100,000 x 6.5/10 years= £65,000;

2. The gain arising by reason of the letting: £100,000 x 2.5*/10 years = £25,000; or

3. £40,000.

The computation of main residence relief would therefore look like this:

	£	£
Gain:		100,000
Less:		
Main residence relief		
£100,000 x 6.5/10	65,000	
Lettings relief	25,000	
Total reliefs:		(90,000)
Chargeable gain:		**10,000**

*Notwithstanding Nancy's main residence being let out for a total of four years, the final 18 months of her period of ownership are relieved in priority and lettings relief is available on a gain which would have been chargeable by reason of the letting, i.e. that relating to two and a half years only.

7.3.2 Lettings relief on a part disposal

Looking at the wording of s. 223(4), it refers to a gain to which s. 222 applies and therefore it is likely to cover a disposal of part of the dwelling-house as well as land which is occupied as gardens or grounds (whether in its entirety or partly). An interesting question arises when as part of a letting arrangement an individual lets out his dwelling-house together with its garden or grounds to tenants, and subsequently disposes of part of the garden land only. On a superficial read, it would be possible to utilise the maximum £40,000 lettings relief several times on numerous disposals of parcels of garden land and this would indicate a need to *pro rata* the relief. However, on a detailed analysis of the provisions of s. 223(4), any "chargeable gain by reason of the letting" would exclusively relate to the part of the dwelling-house or grounds being disposed of which was also let out. In the author's view, the need to utilise the *lower of* the gain arising by reason of the letting, the main residence relief available or £40,000, provides a cap to the lettings relief which obviates the need for a *pro rata* computation.

Law: TCGA 1992, s. 223(1)-(4)

7.4 Lodgers and the "rent-a-room" scheme

According to HMRC's Statement of Practice 14/80 (as it appears in HMRC's Statements of Practice (March 2009)), in cases where the owner of a dwelling-house takes in a lodger who lives as a member of the family, sharing living accommodation and other facilities, no part of the dwelling-house is treated as having ceased to be occupied as the owner's main residence and relief should not be restricted at all. This means that the CGT position is not altered in any way and as long as the entire dwelling-house has been occupied as the owner's only or main residence, relief will continue to apply (as will rent-a-room relief for gross letting income not exceeding £7,500[2]).

In practice, HMRC will not challenge entitlement to lettings relief in respect of a single lodger but draw a specific distinction between these situations and those where the house owner has more than one lodger and equate it to running a lodging house as a business. Whilst this statement could be true depending on the actual facts of a particular case, in the author's view, the existence of two or more lodgers does not in itself render the situation a lodging business. The real question is whether the owner of the dwelling-house has given away exclusive occupation of part of his/her home to the lodgers he or she has taken in. This is ultimately a question of fact to be determined looking at all the facts of the case in the round and a broad-brush approach is likely to find criticism in the First-tier Tribunal.

Guidance: SP 14/80

7.5 Self-contained accommodation and other buildings

HMRC issue a word of warning in respect of lettings of self-contained flats or rooms. SP 14/80 states that in HMRC's view when the owner of a dwelling-house lets out part of it as a flat or set of

---

[2] Before 6 April 2016 the threshold was £4,250.

rooms without structural alterations being effected (irrespective of whether there are separate washing and cooking facilities) letting relief applies without restriction. Conversely, the relief will not extend to former parts of a dwelling-house which have been structurally separated because they are entirely self-contained and have separate street access and would therefore form separate "dwelling-houses".

In contrast, HMRC allow for buildings which are not conventional dwelling-houses (e.g. caravans and parts of industrial units) (see **Chapter 3.4**) to be treated as residences for the purpose of main residence relief. Following this logic, if rooms or parts of these buildings or structures are let out to tenants as residential accommodation, lettings relief should also apply to the proportion of the building and the period of ownership during which they were let out.

Guidance: SP 14/80, CG 64719

7.6 Commercial lettings of furnished holiday accommodation and lettings relief

A property may qualify as "furnished holiday accommodation" within the meaning of ITTOIA 2005, Pt. 3, Ch. 6; TCGA 1992, s. 241, or CTA 2009, Pt. 4, Ch. 6. If such a property is or has been occupied as an individual's only or main residence for any given period of time during the period of ownership, on a strict interpretation of the legislation, a fraction of the gain arising from an eventual disposal of the property could be exempt from CGT according to the principles in TCGA 1992, s. 223(2) (see **6.4** above). If the property is large enough to accommodate its owner(s) and holiday makers at the same time, then the gain could also be restricted by reason of the total area commercially let.

Notwithstanding this, following the Court of Appeal's reasoning in *Owen v Elliott*, lettings relief could also be available for any commercial lettings of holiday accommodation. Owners and advisers should be aware that the availability of lettings relief may, of course, be subject to the terms of the letting being truly commercial and subject to a potential argument of acquisition for the purposes of making a gain under TCGA 1992, s. 224(3).

A further restriction to main residence relief in respect of furnished holiday accommodation is a restriction on rollover relief in situations where:

- a chargeable gain has been deducted under TCGA 1992, s. 152 or 153 from the cost of furnished holiday accommodation; and

- main residence relief applies on the disposal of that accommodation.

On a disposal of a furnished holiday let which has a gain rolled over and has been occupied as an only or main residence, main residence relief is applied and calculated by reference to the chargeable gain which exceeds the gain rolled over (see **Chapter 9** for the interaction between main residence relief and rollover relief).

8. Electing between multiple residences

8.1 Residence vs main residence

S. 222(5) provides a mechanism for determining which of two or more residences is the individual's main residence, as follows:

222. Relief on disposal of private residence

(5) So far as it is necessary for the purposes of this section **to determine which of 2 or more residences is an individual's main residence** for any period—

    (a) **the individual may conclude that question by notice to an officer of the Board given within 2 years** from the beginning of that period but subject to a right to vary that notice by a further notice to an officer of the Board as respects any period beginning not earlier than 2 years before the giving of the further notice.

A few points may be made from a first reading of this subsection:

(i) If an individual has only one residence (regardless of whether it is owned, mortgaged or rented), there can be no question as to which is his only or main residence. It is clearly a matter of fact and ownership of the dwelling-house is not relevant.

(ii) The individual taxpayer has the burden of showing (through available evidence or through an election notice) which of his residences is occupied as the main residence.

(iii) An individual is not compelled to elect the factual main residence; he has a choice as to which residence to elect depending on his plans or circumstances.

(iv) An election will be effective only when it is given in writing or by notice to an officer of HMRC.

(v) There is a right to vary or amend a notice given but statutory time limits apply.

Law: TCGA 1992, s. 222(5)

8.2 Factors to be considered in the absence of an election notice

8.2.1 Introduction

Main residence relief and its intricacies (in particular the existence of elections) are not commonly known to the average home owner. For this reason, it is not altogether rare to find cases where, despite the existence of two or sometimes more residences, there has been no election made in favour of one. In these cases, the factual background and any available evidence will have to be closely considered in order to determine which is as a matter of fact the individual's main residence and for which periods of time. The key factors to be considered are likely to be:

- time spent; and
- quality of occupation.

Each of these is considered below.

8.2.2 Time spent test

The amount of time spent at a particular residence, and the frequency of occupation, should be the initial factors to consider.

In some cases, it will be self-evident that if an individual spends most of his time in a particular residence, it is likely to be his main residence (for example when considering a dwelling-house and a holiday home in the UK or abroad which is used for a few weeks in a year).

In other cases, the number of nights spent in one of two residences may not be decisive. For instance, an individual may have two residences, one of which is a city flat (occupied during the working week) and the other a country house (occupied during the weekends and holidays); in that case, it is not clear-cut whether on a time-spent basis the city flat should be considered the main residence. In practice, the individual may consider the city flat a mere place to stay rather than his residence, in particular if he is there because of work and if his family resides in the country. However, whilst a taxpayer's views or intentions may be taken into account as part of the overall picture, this test is an objective fact-finding exercise which will take into account all relevant factors.

The question as to whether the test of time actually spent in a dwelling-house was conclusive was examined by the High Court in *Frost v Feltham*. Although this case was decided in 1980 and it considered the now defunct mortgage interest relief, it analysed the meaning of the term "only or main residence" as it also featured in the provisions granting that relief.

In that case, there was an appeal by way of case stated from the General Commissioners to the High Court. The Commissioners had agreed with the taxpayer that he was entitled to mortgage interest relief on the purchase of a house in Wales, noting that he "spent some time each month there and all outgoings on the property ... were paid as they fell due". The taxpayer was the publican, tenant and licensee of a public house in Essex and had been for some 17 years. The house in Wales was the only house the taxpayer had ever purchased; it was fully furbished and equipped as a home and, as such, the taxpayer considered it to be his only or main residence. The Revenue disagreed with this finding, arguing that because of the nature of the taxpayer's occupation as a publican, he resided and spent most of his time at the public house so that it had to be regarded as his main residence.

Nourse J. held that the Commissioners had been entitled to find in favour of the taxpayer based on all the evidence they had heard and had not misdirected themselves as to the correct test to be applied in the circumstances. The learned judge also held that:

> "If someone lives in two houses the question, which does he use as the principal or more important one [main residence], cannot be determined solely by reference to the way in which he divides his time between the two."

In other words, periods of time spent in a residence do not provide a conclusive answer to the much broader factual question of main residence. In the author's view, a common sense approach should be taken by HMRC officers (and ultimately by the tax tribunals) when reviewing an election notice or a claim for the main residence exemption. The pertinent case law on this subject certainly indicates that such an approach, if reasonable, will not be overturned by the higher courts.

Case: *Frost v Feltham* [1981] STC 115

8.2.3   Quality of occupation

In finding whether a residence has in fact been occupied as a person's "settled living place", it would also be helpful to consider and compare the individual's treatment of the residence. "Treatment" in this context refers to whether the person regards the residence as his one and true home. HMRC state (at CG 64545) that this could be determined by looking at a series of questions:

- If the individual is married or in a civil partnership, where does the family spend its time?
- If the individual has children, where do they go to school?
- At which residence is the individual registered to vote?
- Where is the individual's place of work?
- How is each residence furnished?
- Which address is used for correspondence?
    - Banks & Building Societies
    - Credit cards
    - HMRC
- Where is the individual registered with a doctor / dentist?
- At which address is the individual's car registered and insured?
- Which address is the main residence for council tax?

Although this list of question is not intended to be exhaustive, the property which appears as the answer to most of these questions is likely to be the individual's main residence (unless there are other significant factors which point the other way). For a recent case where the taxpayer presented a good paper trail but failed to convince the Tribunal of his quality of occupation see *Oliver v HMRC* (full analysis at **2.3.9** above).

Case: *Oliver v HMRC* [2016] UKFTT 796 (TC)
Guidance: CG 64545

8.3   Election notices

8.3.1   Introduction

As set out in **8.1** above, in cases where there are two or more residences, an individual has a wide discretion to nominate one of them (regardless of actual occupation) to be treated as his main residence for the purposes of main residence relief (TCGA 1992, s. 222(5)(a)). In former s. 222(5)(b), which was repealed by FA 1996 with effect from the tax year 1996/97 (the introduction of self-assessment), the ability to make an election for main residence relief was restricted by the requirement of a final determination by an inspector which may have related to the whole or part of the period of ownership in question. The repeal of s. 222(5)(b) in 1996 means that as long as a notice of election is valid and sent within the specified time limits, it will be conclusive in favour of the residence nominated. There will be no scope for challenge from HMRC (unless there is doubt as to whether the dwelling-house in question has been occupied as a residence). The repealed section is considered further at **8.3.3** below.

8.3.2   Form of notice

There is no specific statutory form prescribed for an election notice. The legislation simply requires that:

(i)   notice must be given (in writing or otherwise, but bearing in mind the burden of proof which rests on a taxpayer); and

(ii)   a notice should be given to an officer of the Board but it does not specify location or grade of officer.

HMRC provide clarification on this point at CG 64520. According to that guidance, the following conditions must be fulfilled:

- A nomination by an individual must be made to an officer of the Board and must be signed by the individual.

- Spouses or civil partners who are living together can only have one main residence between them for the purpose of private residence relief. If a nomination affects both of them it must be made by notice in writing to an officer of the Board and must be signed by both of them.

137

- Where one of more of the residences is occupied by a person entitled to occupy it under the terms of a settlement, the notice must be writing to an officer of the Board and should be signed by both the trustees of the settlement and the person entitled to occupy the residence.
- The signature of an agent is not sufficient.

The author can find no justification for these conditions imposed by HMRC (in statute or cases). Having said that, and in order to avoid potential investigations or disputes with HMRC, adherence to these requirements is considered prudent. As a matter of good professional conduct, advisers should ensure that a copy of the final notice sent to HMRC is kept in the taxpayer's file in case the notice is lost or destroyed whilst in HMRC's hands.

8.3.3 Time limits

To analyse properly the effect of the time limits for giving an election notice, it is necessary to look closely at the current version of s. 222(5):

> "(5) So far as it is necessary for the purposes of this section to determine which of 2 or more residences is an individual's main residence for **any period**—
>
> > (a) the individual may conclude that question by notice to an officer of the Board given **within** 2 years from the beginning of **that period** but subject to a **right to vary** that notice by a further notice to an officer of the Board as respects **any period** beginning **not earlier than 2 years before** the giving of the further notice."

> (emphasis added)

As mentioned above, s. 222(5) was "cut in half" with the introduction of self-assessment in 1996 and s. 222(5)(b) and the words following it, were repealed in their totality. Former s. 222(5)(b) read as follows:

> "(b) subject to paragraph (a) above, the question shall be concluded by the determination of the inspector, which may be as respects **the whole or specified parts of the period of ownership in question,**

and notice of any determination of the inspector under paragraph (b) above shall be given to the individual who may appeal to the General Commissioners or the Special Commissioners against that determination within 30 days of service of the notice."

(emphasis again added)

Former s. 222(5)(b) is mentioned here because its wording was heavily relied upon by the High Court in *Craig-Harvey* in order to interpret s. 222(5)(a) as requiring taxpayers to give an election notice within 2 years of *acquiring* a second residence.

Law: TCGA 1992, s. 222(5)

Griffin v Craig-Harvey

In that case, the taxpayer, Mr Craig-Harvey owned three properties in the period between November 1981 and 26 January 1989. The first, Balldown Farmhouse, was acquired as a gift from his father on 12 August 1985 and sold on 26 January 1989. The second, Stockwell Park Crescent, was bought in 1981 and contracts for sale were exchanged on 17 April 1986, with completion on 9 July 1986. On the same date, the taxpayer completed on a third property, Sibella Road.

The question for the Special Commissioners to consider was whether a notice of election given more than two years after the acquisition of the Farmhouse was valid. The taxpayer argued, and the Commissioners accepted, that the words in CGTA 1979, s. 101(5)(a) (an almost identical precursor to s. 222(5)(a)) "from the beginning of that period" related back to the words "for any period" in the opening of the section. As a consequence, it was argued that there was no restriction – express or implied – on the date chosen as the beginning of that period and an election notice may be given at any time.

The Revenue argued that a valid notice of election had to be given within two years of the date of the taxpayer's acquisition of a new residence or making a change in residence. In that case, the notice that the Farmhouse should be treated as a main residence had to be given within two years of the date of sale of Stockwell Park and purchase of Sibella Road.

In the alternative, the Revenue argued that if the wording of CGTA 1979, s. 101(5) was ambiguous or obscure, reference could be made to *Hansard* debates concerning the *Finance (No. 2) Bill* 1965 as an aid to construction under the principles in *Pepper v Hart*. During the relevant Parliamentary debate, the Financial Secretary was recorded as saying that the effect of minor amendments to the section[1] was to "keep open the option so that [an individual] can exercise a choice within two years from the time when he acquires the second house".

Vinelott J held that the existence of s. 101(5)(b) (latterly s. 222(5)(b)) could not be ignored. In fact, in the learned judge's view, paragraph (a), though it came first, was in substance an exception from the general rule set out in paragraph (b), namely that where there was a question of which of two residences was an individual's main residence as respects the whole or specified parts of the period of ownership in question, that question had to be decided by the inspector. The taxpayer then had the right to appeal that decision and the right to "conclude that question" – i.e. the question to be determined by the inspector – by way of an election notice. The learned judge added that the words "any period" and "that period" were most naturally read as referring to "the whole or any part of the period of ownership in question".

Dealing with the point on any ambiguity of the provisions and the parliamentary debates, Vinelott J held first, that there was no ambiguity or obscurity and secondly that even if there were, the statement by the Financial Secretary put the matter beyond doubt. There is a strong argument to suggest that the observations made by the Financial Secretary to Parliament were purely directed at the specific amendments proposed and that there was no contemplation of backdated notices or of when the two-year limit should start. With respect, the Court's interpretation of the statement seems misdirected and the context of the debate does not support the conclusion reached.

---

[1] The first amendment was the insertion in the opening words of subsection (7) (now s. 222(5)) of the words "for any period" after the words "an individual's main residence". The second was the substitution of the words "beginning of that period" for the words "date of the acquisition of, or of his original interest in, the dwelling-house or part of the dwelling-house which is treated by the Notice as his main..."

In the author's view, a straightforward reading of TCGA 1992, s. 222(5)(a) renders the conclusion reached by the Court, at best, unsafe. It is suggested that the words "any period" in s. 222(5) refer to any period of time when the selection between two (or more) properties that are being occupied as residences by an individual must be made for the purposes of exemption (in other words when the need arises to elect between two dwelling-houses which are occupied as residences). It would defy logic to invoke a provision to determine / elect a main residence in a situation where despite ownership, there is no second "residence" because a second dwelling-house simply does not hold that status (e.g. the second dwelling could be in the process of refurbishment, or it could lack all amenities and furniture or simply remain unoccupied).

In the circumstances there is a strong argument to suggest that *Craig-Harvey* was wrongly decided for several reasons and that the two-year limit in s. 222(5) starts to run from the date two or more dwelling-houses are occupied as residences.

As a matter of good practice and good planning, any elections should be made as soon as possible and, in any event, within two years of acquisition of the second home or any relevant change in circumstances. If a taxpayer misses this time limit, there are two options available: the first would be to argue that the legal precedent of *Craig-Harvey* was incorrectly decided and the second may be the application of an extra-statutory concession.

Cases: *Pepper v Hart* [1993] AC 593; *Griffin (Inspector of Taxes) v Craig-Harvey* (1994) 66 TC 396, [1994] BTC 3

8.3.4   Recent case on elections

Munford v HMRC

In June 2004, Mr and Mrs Munford bought a dwelling-house in NW11 London for £4m. On the same day, Mr Munford purchased another dwelling-house in SW3 London in his sole name for £1.05m. The second property required full renovation and works started in late 2004. The same property was eventually sold on 21 March 2006 for £2.55m.

Two and a half weeks prior to the sale of the SW3 property, Mr Munford's agents made an election to treat the NW11 house as the family's main residence with effect from June 2004. One week later they switched their election to treat the SW3 property as their main residence with effect from 19 December 2015. One week after that there was a further switch to treat the NW11 house as Mr Munford's main residence. At the time of the Tribunal appeal, the taxpayers continued to occupy the latter property as their main residence.

HMRC started to enquire into Mr Munford's 2006 tax return in 2013 after information received from Kensington & Chelsea Borough Council "very much suggested that Mr Munford and family had never moved into the property". HMRC issued a discovery assessment on the basis of deliberate conduct and a penalty of nearly £190,000 (65% of the assessed tax).

The taxpayer argued, and the FTT agreed, that the family had intended to move to the SW3 London property which was a five-storey town house with four bedrooms. The taxpayers had considered this to be the correct size for them and their two children. In 2004, they had no intention of having any more children. The renovation project had taken a long time to complete because they were creating what they thought would be the ideal family home. The second (and more expensive) property had been bought for a very good price and the family intended to live there whilst the building works were being carried out at their intended final home. The intention was to sell the second house once they could move into their newly refurbished home.

The family eventually moved into the SW3 London property in November 2005 whilst there were still snagging issues to be resolved but hoping this would prompt the builders to complete all works sooner rather than later. At the beginning, the family had mattresses on the floor and their bedding only, and asserted that they did not find this a hardship as they were due to go away on holiday for Christmas. Mrs Munford had unexpectedly fallen pregnant and was four months along when they moved into the new house. The expected arrival of their third child made them re-think their decision to move to the SW3 property as it was a town house with many stairs and not practical for a new born baby. When they were on holiday they had decided to move into the NW11 house as it was considerably bigger and would more suitable for a baby/ toddler and a live-in nanny. They moved out on their return on 6 January 2006.

The FTT held that the plan to renovate the property was consistent with the taxpayers' intention to reside there permanently as a family. Further, the lack of notification to the Council of their brief move to the property (or any others) was not inconsistent with their swift decision to move out whilst they were on holiday. The FTT did not give much weight to the lack of furniture at the property and found that HMRC had failed to show on the balance of probabilities that the family had not occupied the house as their residence for a short period of time. The FTT mentioned that if the burden of proof had been on the taxpayers, their decision may well have been different.

On the question of the timings of the various elections made by Mr Munford, the FTT agreed with the appellant that the elections were definitive and that there was no reason why the periods of election should correspond exactly or at all with the periods of actual occupation. The fact that one election had been for one week only did not assist on the fact-finding exercise to be carried out by the Tribunal.

Case: *Munford v HMRC* [2017] UKFTT 19 (TC)

Harrison v HMRC

The main issue to be decided in this case was whether or not main residence relief was due on the sale of six properties (a number which on the day of the hearing was conceded by the taxpayer to four) disposed of by the taxpayer during the tax years 2009-10 and 2010-11.

The chronology of ownership of the properties was complex and, during the hearing, it became clear that at least two of the properties were located in the same apartment building.

The taxpayer resided in a farmhouse which he admitted was his main residence but argued that other properties were second homes that became main residences by way of elections.

The FTT held that an election under s. 222(5)(a) is only effective between two *only or main* main residences. The making of an election could not transform a property into an only or main residence. In the Tribunal's view, there was a requirement to occupy the property as a residence with a sufficient degree of permanence and continuity, otherwise any election would be bound to fail.

143

The author notes the FTT's comments to the effect that an election must be made between two *only or main* residences rather than two *residences*. Such an interpretation of the rule in s. 222(5)(a) would be plainly wrong and contrary to the established case law. It is likely, however, that this was a mere slip in the decision. First, the FTT set out the wording of s. 222 in full in the law section of the decision and second, the FTT concluded that:

> "the quality of the appellant's occupation of his second homes – the degree of permanence, the degree of continuity or the expectation of continuity – was not such as to amount to 'residence' within the meaning of section 222 TCGA. It is very clear that his home and therefore his established main residence at all material times was his farmhouse."

This passage clearly demonstrates an understanding of the differences in law between the terms "residence" and "main residence".

With regards to the taxpayer's contention that HMRC had (incorrectly) accepted a claim for main residence relief in respect of an earlier investigation, the FTT held that this did not mean it should be done in respect of any of the other years in question. The appeal was refused.

Case: *Harrison v HMRC* [2015] UKFTT 539 (TC)

Ellis v HMRC

The case of *Ellis* was decided in December 2012 after a contested hearing before the First-tier Tribunal. The case involved a property purchased in March 1999 which was continuously let until 31 August 2004. The appellant argued that she and her late husband had decided to use the property as a residence from the beginning of October 2004. An election notice under s. 222(5) had been sent to HMRC on 29 October 2004 and was acknowledged on 22 November 2004.

Following disposal of the property on 13 April 2005, HMRC opened an enquiry in May 2008, arguing that the property had not been occupied as a residence. However, by the time the case got to the tribunal, HMRC had changed their line of attack, challenging whether the property was used a *main* residence.

With the existence of a valid election notice, the tribunal found:

> "... given that the respondents [HMRC] concede that the property was a residence used by the taxpayers, the appeals must succeed because an election was made. The respondents cannot go behind the election ... ."

This decision confirms the established position that a valid and timely notice of election is conclusive of the question of main residence whether HMRC like it or not.

Case: *Ellis and another v HMRC* [2013] UKFTT 3 (TC)

8.4   Extension of time limits in certain cases

According to Extra-Statutory Concession D21, the two-year time limit set in the legislation may be waived or extended in particular circumstances, as follows:

> "Where for any period an individual has, or is treated by the Taxes Acts as having more than one residence, but his interest in each of them, or in each of them except one, is such as to have no more than a negligible capital value on the open market (e.g. a weekly rented flat, or accommodation provided by an employer) the two year time limit laid down by section 222(5)(a), TCGA 1992 for nominating one of those residences as the individuals main residence for capital gains tax purposes will be extended where the individual was unaware that such a nomination could be made. In such cases the nomination may be made within a reasonable time of the individual first becoming aware of the possibility of making a nomination, and it will be regarded as effective from the date on which the individual first had more than one residence."

This concession will provide comfort to taxpayers who inadvertently miss the deadline for nomination of a main residence in circumstances where their second home is subject to a very short licence or lease, or if it is provided by their employer. It should be noted, however, that the concession is very narrowly drafted and that it is unlikely to cover longer rental arrangements like an assured shorthold tenancy and accommodation obtained because of a job placement but not provided directly by an employer. It is also unclear as to whether or not the concession could be used in a situation after a disposal of a second residence has been completed but where the objective awareness of the possibility of a nomination comes afterwards.

Guidance: ESC D21

8.5 Elections for married couples and civil partners

According to TCGA 1992, s. 222(6):

> "In the case of an individual living with his spouse or civil partner —
>
> > (a) there can only be one residence or main residence for both, so long as living together and, where a notice under subsection (5)(a) above affects both the individual and his spouse or civil partner, it must be given by both."

There can only be one main residence and one notice of election in the case of spouses or civil partners. Apart from the fact that this provision is clearly discriminatory to couples who are legally bound in a relationship, and therefore it represents an inequality likely to be in breach of human rights, there is no elucidation of what the term "living together" means in the legislation or guidance and it seems that it would depend on the particular facts of each case.

This lack of definition in s. 222(6) has the potential to create uncertainty in cases where there is temporary separation of a relationship (which may or may not result in one of the parties moving out of the joint home) and it is unclear as to whether the couple was "living together" for the purposes of the legislation.

It is recommended that in cases where there is in fact a separation which leads to a party moving out and taking residence in another dwelling-house, clear and contemporaneous evidence is kept to show that there was an intention and an actual occupation of a second home for the relevant period of time.

It would seem that the two-year limit for making an election in these cases will start to run from the date of registration of marriage or civil partnership and that a single notice of election signed by both individuals will be required only when it will affect both parties.

Law: TCGA 1992, s. 222(6)
Guidance: CG 64525

8.6 Changes to elections – non-resident CGT on disposals of UK residences

As we have seen, an individual with two or more residences for any given period of time may elect by notice under s. 222(5)(a) for one of those residences to be his main residence. New s. 222(6A) provides that that election cannot be disturbed or voided by the fact that during the same period another residence is treated as not being occupied as a residence for a tax year under the terms of new s. 222B (residence located in a territory in which the individual is not tax resident and the day count test is not satisfied). All of these changes apply to disposals made on or after 6 April 2015.

A dwelling-house (or part thereof) is treated as not being occupied as a residence by an individual at any time during the ownership period if that period falls within a non-qualifying tax year or a non-qualifying partial tax year (TCGA 1992, s. 222B).

A "non-qualifying year" is defined as a tax year which falls within an individual's period of ownership and:

(1) the individual (or his spouse / civil partner) was not resident for tax purposes in the country in which the dwelling-house is situated; and

(2) the individual (or his spouse / civil partner) has not stayed overnight at the relevant dwelling-house(s) for at least 90 non-consecutive days during the year ("day count test") (TCGA 1992, s. 222C).

Where the dwelling-house is owned for part of a year, the day count test is reduced by a proportionate amount. If more than one residence is owned in the same country during that part of the year, the number of nights spent in each residence may be aggregated. Furthermore, the day count test does not prevent allowable absences applying in respect of a non-qualifying year. (See **2.5** above for further detail).

147

In addition, new TCGA 1992, s. 222A provides that when an individual makes a disposal of a UK residence whilst non-resident for tax purposes, any election must be made in a non-resident tax return (as prescribed by HMRC). Such an election may vary the terms of an election notice previously given under s. 222(5)(a) in respect of any period of ownership except for a notice in respect of a residence that has already been disposed of (in whole or in part). It is important to note that despite an ability to amend a previous election notice under s. 222(5)(a), a non-resident CGT disposal election notice is in itself not subject to variation (TCGA 1992, s. 222A(6)).

Law: FA 2015, Sch. 9; TCGA 1992, s. 222(6A), 222A, 222B, 222C

8.7 Planning opportunities

It may seem like an obvious point but the first thing that an adviser (or residence owner) should do is become familiar with the possibility of making a main residence election. Familiarity with the rules would enable a taxpayer to decide which property should be elected depending on his circumstances and any foreseeable future plans. In many cases elections are overlooked (and CGT incurred) simply because the client is unaware of the choice.

In cases where the time limits for an election have been missed and the time spent test is not strictly met, the onus would be on the individual to show that, as a matter of fact, the dwelling-house is his actual main residence (despite the individual spending more time elsewhere). In order to discharge this burden, the individual should ensure that a close link with the residence is maintained at all relevant times. This may be done by demonstrating that this would be the place where the individual would spend the entirety of his time "if he had a choice".

For the willing client, there are other ways of mitigating the effect of an overlooked election. A possibility would be for the client to obtain a further (or in most cases, third) residence. As long as the new dwelling-house is occupied as a residence, then the time limit for a main residence election (according to HMRC's guidance and *Craig-Harvey*) would restart. A clear advantage here is that the new property need not be owned by the individual, as residence is not dependent on ownership, and that a short-term lease (but not a mere licence[2]) would suffice.

The fact that the individual has a newly occupied residence will then enable him to nominate any of the three dwelling-houses as a main residence. It is vital to remember that in order to nominate any dwelling-house, it must be occupied as a residence (see **8.2.2** above).

A second possibility for mitigation would be for the individual to let out one of the two residences in question for a relatively short period of time. This will have the effect of cutting ties, getting rid of "an interest" in the property and decreasing the number of dwelling-houses available to be occupied as a residence. At the end of the tenancy, the dwelling-house becomes a dwelling-house which may qualify as a residence afresh and an election in favour of the desired main residence may then be made.

Variation of election notices and allowable absences (last 18 months of ownership)

This type of planning has become less attractive since the reduction of the deemed period of occupation of a main residence from the last 36 months of the ownership period to the last 18 months, but in some cases it is still worth considering.

Pursuant to s. 222(5)(a), an individual has a statutory right to vary a notice of election retrospectively for up to two years prior in the ownership period. When this right is coupled with the statutory allowable absence covering the last 18 months of the ownership period (irrespective of how long the property holds main residence status), it may provide a helpful way of mitigating short-term CGT on the disposal of a residence.

This type of planning is best illustrated by way of an example:

Example

Kevin owns two residences – Temple Mews and Hayfield Cottage – and has occupied them as residences since 1995. In 2000, he nominated Hayfield Cottage as his main residence. On 3 April 2015,

---

[2] For guidance on election notices made in favour of residences occupied under a mere licence see CG 64536. HMRC treat such notices given after 16 October 1994 as invalid.

he receives an offer too good to ignore for the sale of Temple Mews and disposes of it realising a significant capital gain. It is clear that as matters stand, the gain accrued on Temple Mews will not benefit from main residence relief unless the election made in favour of Hayfield Cottage is varied.

On 3 May 2015, after advice received from his accountants, Kevin submits a notice of variation under s. 222(5)(a) of the original election, changing it to benefit Temple Mews. This variation is backdated to 3 May 2013. The effect of this election would be to treat Temple Mews as Kevin's main residence for a period of time in 2013. Kevin may then flip his election back to Hayfield Cottage in a relatively short space of time (a week or two afterwards). The end result of this election "flip" is that Kevin will be able to claim main residence relief (and potentially a maximum of £40,000 lettings relief) on the disposal of Temple Mews for the last 18 months of ownership, from 3 October 2013 to 3 April 2015.

The only downside of this planning is the loss of main residence relief on the actual main residence, Hayfield Cottage, for one or two weeks of the ownership period. The significant relief gained on the disposal of Temple Mews is likely to compensate for this loss of relief even in cases where the annual exemption could not cover it.

The author suggests that the first and second variations are not combined into one single election notice to avoid the real risk that HMRC will treat the variation as invalid.

Law: TCGA 1992, s. 222(5)(a), 223

Case: *Griffin (Inspector of Taxes) v Craig-Harvey* (1994) 66 TC 396, [1994] BTC 3

Guidance: CG 64510, 64536

9.   Restrictions on relief

9.1   Overview

TCGA 1992, s. 224 introduces further restrictions on the amount of main residence relief that an individual may claim, as follows:

- exclusive business use;
- a change of what is occupied as a dwelling-house (reconstructions, conversions or any other reason); and
- acquisition made wholly or partly for the purpose of realising a capital gain.

9.2   Business use

9.2.1   Introduction

TCGA 1992, s. 224(1) provides that in the case of a dwelling-house (or part thereof) that is used *exclusively* for the purpose of a trade, business, profession or vocation any capital gain which accrues on a subsequent disposal shall be apportioned into:

- gain eligible for main residence relief (for which the main residence exemption will apply); and
- gain which is not exempt.

The said apportionment is made in relation to the use made of the dwelling-house in question but it is not the same test as the "wholly and exclusively" test which must be fulfilled in order to determine whether an expense is allowable in calculating the taxable profits of a trade or business.

If any given room in a dwelling-house is used partly for business and partly as a residence, then the entire accrued gain will be eligible for main residence relief. The key word in the legislation is "exclusively" and this establishes that the restriction is limited to rooms or spaces in a dwelling-house where the private or residence use is *de minimis*.

HMRC contend that private use versus business use apportionments will be appropriate where part of a dwelling-house has been used exclusively for trade or business purposes *throughout* the entire period of ownership. If this is the case, main residence relief will be denied for the duration and the last 18 months of ownership would not be exempt.

9.2.2 Home office

In the case of a person who uses a room in his dwelling-house as a study or office for the purposes of his trade, business, profession or vocation, main residence relief would still be available on this part of the residence if the room is also used for domestic purposes (reading, family finances, streaming or watching videos) – even if expenses of running the office have been deducted from business taxable profits. Conversely, main residence relief may still be refused if the office is used exclusively for business purposes, even if no deduction for business expenses has been made. Clients and advisers should be aware of this potential trap and decide whether the need for exclusivity of business use outweighs the loss of main residence relief.

9.2.3 Apportionment

HMRC guidance refers to the question of how much of a capital gain should be apportioned to residential use and how much should be apportioned to business use as a matter of fact to be decided depending on the circumstances of each case. Although there are no hard and fast rules of apportionment, HMRC suggest that:

> "In a mixed property, such as a public house with residential accommodation above, the business part would be expected to be of greater value than the residential. So an apportionment based solely on the number of rooms or the floor area used for each purpose could produce an excessive amount of relief. In small cases any reasonable apportionment may be accepted. If the tax at stake is material or the apportionment appears to have been unduly weighted in favour of the residential accommodation the Valuation Office Agency should be consulted."

In the main, HMRC also seem to object to an apportionment based on two separate assets: a dwelling-house and a business property. The distinction between a mixed property and two separate assets lies on the apportionment of consideration. If the business part of a dwelling-house is treated as a separate asset, an apportionment of expenditure and consideration must be made in relation to it; whereas if the business part is treated as part of the dwelling-house, any apportionment is made as the last stage of a tax computation. This may make a significant difference for the individual who has expended significant sums on the business part and who could claim an allowable loss if this part was treated as a second asset.

HMRC argue that "such an approach is not a proper apportionment and will produce an excessive amount of relief."

Law: TCGA 1992, s. 224(1)
Guidance: CG 64670

9.2.4   Farmhouses

Whether or not a farmhouse is used exclusively for the purposes of a farm business is also a matter of fact. Notwithstanding this, as long as the farmhouse has been occupied as a residence by the farmer and his family, there should be no restriction of main residence relief. An apportionment of relief would not be made unless a part of the farmhouse has been used exclusively for business purposes (for example as an office or dairy, or as storage of produce).

Guidance: CG 64680

9.2.5   Interaction with rollover relief

If, in any given case, main residence relief is not available in respect of part of a dwelling-house used exclusively for the purpose of a trade or business, then in theory, rollover relief under TCGA 1992, s. 152(5) or (6) may be available. If a replacement business property is purchased then the gain accrued on the part of the dwelling-house used exclusively for business may be deferred until a future sale.

In appropriate cases, there may be an opportunity to use both main residence relief and rollover relief because there is no requirement to use a replacement business property for the purposes of the business for the entire period of ownership.

Example

Suki has run a successful acupuncture practice (one room and hallway used as waiting area) from her home in Staines since 2002. Her tax adviser has informed her that this business use would mean a restriction of main residence relief of 20% on any accrued gain. She was offered a place at a brand new private holistic clinic in Birmingham and has decided to sell her house, relocate to Birmingham and move her practice to the clinic. This being the case, she will not have a replacement business property in which to roll over her restricted gain.

A planning opportunity would be to relocate to Birmingham before the clinic is completed and continue to practise from her new home as she has done thus far. This would enable her to defer 20% of the gain accrued on her former dwelling-house into the new residence. Once the clinic is ready she may move without the cessation of business occupation of her new home triggering any tax liability. If the Birmingham dwelling-house is not disposed of, the deferred gain may never be clawed back or become chargeable. In the event of a disposal, and depending on the period of ownership, a few months of exclusive business use would mean a very modest apportionment pursuant to TCGA 1992, s. 224(2).

Furnished holiday lettings

A chargeable gain may be rolled over into an FHL property which is subsequently occupied as a main or only residence by a person. In that case, main residence relief is restricted to that part of the chargeable gain which exceeds the amount of the gain rolled over.

For an example on how to compute the chargeable gain see CG 61452.

Compulsory purchase orders (CPO)

The *Town and Country Planning Act* 1990 grants powers to the Secretary of State and local planning authorities to make orders for the acquisition of private land and buildings for planning and public purposes. The most common situation when a dwelling-house would be included in a CPO would be for a major infrastructure project, for gas or oil extraction, or for the construction of a highway or train line.

In a case where a landowner (including individuals, trustees or companies) is confronted with a CPO and has to dispose of his dwelling-house through this statutory provision, the CGT treatment is beneficial.

154

TCGA 1992, s. 247 provides that for land disposed of (or severance compensation paid) on or after 6 April 1982, if there is a replacement land or property (which is not excluded), the landowner may roll the accrued gain on the disposal into the replacement land. This relief is modelled on rollover relief for replacement of business assets.

There is, however, a catch. TCGA 192, s. 248 excludes a replacement dwelling-house if it is occupied as an only or main residence and denies rollover relief if it is sold within six years of the original purchase. This provision ensures that a capital gain made on a compulsory acquisition and rolled over into a dwelling-house comes back into charge within six years.

Law: TCGA 1992, s. 247, 248
Guidance: CG 61900ff.

9.2.6   Interaction with holdover relief

Similarly to roll over relief, if an individual has been carrying on a furnished holiday letting business from a dwelling-house which is then transferred as a gift to a family member, there is potential for a claim for holdover relief pursuant to TCGA 1992, s. 165. If that family member decides to occupy the dwelling-house as his main or only residence, he may be able to claim full main residence relief on a subsequent disposal.

This would, in effect, mean that a disposal of an FHL business could be rendered entirely CGT exempt. As long as:

- the disposals are genuine;
- all the conditions for holdover relief are satisfied; and
- the dwelling-house is occupied as a main residence with an intention to occupy permanently,

there should be little scope for challenge from HMRC.

Law: TCGA 1992, s. 165, 222

9.2.7   Interaction with entrepreneurs' relief

In a simple case where part of a dwelling-house has been used exclusively for business purposes and part has been occupied as an only or main residence, s. 224 provides for main residence relief for the part so occupied and a chargeable gain accruing in respect of the part used for business purposes. A just and reasonable apportionment of relief should also be made. See **9.3** below.

If the dwelling-house is disposed of at the same time as a material disposal of a business (or within three years of the business cessation), a chargeable gain accruing on the non-residential part may attract entrepreneurs' relief.

Advisers should be alive to the strict conditions for entitlement to entrepreneurs' relief, to the lifetime limit of £10m and to the requirement to make a formal claim for the relief on or before the first anniversary of the 31 January following the tax year in which the qualifying business disposal is made. This is in stark contrast with main residence relief where no claim is necessary[1] and where there is no limit on the amount of relief.

9.3   Changes of use and apportionment

TCGA 1992, s. 224(2) provides:

> "If at any time in the period of ownership there is a change in what is occupied as the individual's residence, whether on account of a **reconstruction or conversion of a building** or for any other reason, **or there have been changes as regards the use of part of the dwelling-house for the purpose of a trade or business, or of a profession or vocation**, or for any other purpose, **the relief given** by section 223 **may be adjusted** in a manner which is **just and reasonable**."

In essence, s. 224(2) dictates that a just and reasonable apportionment of main residence relief must be made in circumstances where there is a change of use (from residential to business), where the dwelling has been substantially reconstructed or converted into smaller units or for any other reason. Its scope is wide and it directly affects the amount of relief due under TCGA 1992, s. 223.

Any apportionment computation should take into account the floor space, rooms or extent to which the dwelling-house was occupied as a residence *and* the period of time (compared to the period of

---

[1] Unless the garden or grounds exceed the permitted area of 0.5ha.

ownership) during which the dwelling-house was a main or only residence.

It should be noted that if any part of a dwelling-house (regardless of its size) has been occupied as a main residence at any stage of the ownership period, main residence relief should be available for the last 18 months of the ownership period in relation to that part.

HMRC guidance warns that an adjustment under s. 224(2) is not appropriate where the change of use occurs when the dwelling-house begins or ceases to be used as a residence. The method of computing relief in such circumstances is provided by TCGA 1992, s. 223(2) and there is therefore no need for an adjustment to the relief.

The question of correct apportionment in s. 224 is ultimately a matter of valuation evidence. In cases where apportionment is at issue, it is not uncommon for HMRC to instruct the Valuation Office Agency ("VoA") to provide an opinion as to the correct method of valuation. Indeed, the VoA has extensive guidance on these matters – see VOA *Technical Capital Gains Tax Manual* online.

For an example of how the question of apportionment was resolved by the Upper Tribunal (Lands Chamber) see the decision in *Oates v HMRC*. In this case, the Judge disagreed with the "just and reasonable" apportionment of value between a house and adjoining land which had been used by a senior valuer for the VoA. The Tribunal held that arriving at the value of a dwelling-house based upon its existing use, whilst ignoring the development value, would inappropriately apportion all of the development value to the land, depriving the taxpayers of potential main residence relief. The Upper Tribunal tested the taxpayer's given value for the dwelling-house against two possible methods of apportionment and concluded that the valuation was within a reasonable range.

Law: TCGA 1992, s. 223, 224(2)

Case: *Oates v HMRC* [2014] UKUT 409 (LC)

Guidance: CG 64767; Valuation Office Agency's technical manual used to assess CGT and other taxes

157

9.4 Acquisition made for the purpose of a gain

9.4.1 Overview

A further limitation to the amount of main residence relief which may be obtained on the disposal of a residence comes in the form of TCGA 1992, s. 224(3). This provision disapplies main residence relief in cases where a disposal of a dwelling-house or an interest in a dwelling-house has been made wholly or partly for the aim of realising a capital gain (see **9.4.2** and **9.4.3** below).

Further, any gain will fall outside the exemption too if it is attributable to expenditure which has been incurred:

- after the beginning of the period of ownership; and
- with the same aim.

The second part of s. 224(3) (see **9.4.4** below) is invoked more often by HMRC and usually in respect of an acquisition by a leaseholder of a superior interest in the property or the conversion of the dwelling-house into flats.

The restriction in s. 224(3) is designed to honour the wishes of Parliament conveyed when CGT was first introduced in 1962 (see **1.2.1** above for a history of its inception). The Government's pledge was to introduce a new tax on capital which would not extend to owner-occupied dwellings. It is therefore clear that any property investment ventures, speculative gains or property developments would be clearly outside the scope of the exemption.

The first thing to consider is whether or not a dwelling-house has been acquired as part of a trade or venture in the nature of a trade and whether income tax should be chargeable on any resulting profits (see **6.1** above). That being the case, CGT and main residence relief will become irrelevant.

In practice, if a tax return is under enquiry, HMRC tend to issue closure notices in the alternative: on the one hand alleging that the person acquired and disposed of the dwelling-house in the course of a trade or venture in the nature of a trade and on the other hand that he or she made a disposal for the purpose of realising a gain under s. 224(3). The author was involved in a case where HMRC had amended a self-assessment on the basis of trading income and failed to assess to CGT in the alternative. When HMRC eventually became aware of their error – near the time of an appeal hearing – they tried to issue an amended closure notice but the First-tier Tribunal rejected their application on the grounds of undue delay and prejudice to the taxpayer. In the author's view, similar attempts to correct such an oversight by HMRC should be strongly resisted.

Law: TCGA 1992, s. 224(3)
Guidance: CG 65200ff.

9.4.2 Residence acquired for whole purpose of realising a gain (first limb of s. 224(3))

In cases where a dwelling-house is bought with the sole intention of investing and realising a short or long-term gain there may be one of two outcomes.

First, if the dwelling-house is not occupied as a main residence, then any gain realised would be fully chargeable to CGT.

Second, if the dwelling-house is in fact occupied as a main residence for some of the period of ownership, the full effect of TCGA 1992, s. 224(3) is to deny main residence relief on the entire gain regardless of any periods of occupation as a residence.

In practice it is always a matter of fact whether the purchase of a dwelling-house was only motivated by a desire to realise a gain. The total period of ownership, extent of occupation and amount of gain may be helpful indicators to assist a Tribunal to decide if the gain is exempt or not.

9.4.3 Residence acquired partly for purpose of realising a gain (first limb of s. 224(3))

In cases where a purchase of a dwelling-house has been made for dual or composite motives, one of which is the likelihood of appreciation and a desire to realise a gain, the full effect of s. 224(3) is also to deny main residence relief on the entire gain regardless of periods of occupation as a main residence.

Again, whether the second part of the first limb applies is a question of fact and the evidential burden would fall on the owner of the dwelling-house to show that the intention to realise a gain was inconsequential and not the driving force for the purchase. Factors like transport links or proximity to a work place, school catchment areas and access to amenities may be helpful evidence to show that appreciation was incidental to the main purpose of owning a residence in a particular location.

In the author's experience, an argument that the restriction in s. 224(3) applies to the disposal of a dwelling-house usually comes as an alternative to a trading argument and predominantly in the case of builders, property developers and those working in the construction industry (architects, surveyors and construction managers). It should be noted that the owner-occupier's profession, trade or business is by no means conclusive and cases must be looked at in the round. There are many genuine cases where owners simply change their minds on a property very shortly after purchase and decide to move relatively quickly whilst at the same time realising a profit. If there is cogent evidence to demonstrate that this is indeed the case, full main residence relief ought to be available.

Finally, it should be noted that the word "purpose" in the legislation suggests a requirement for the person concerned to have an intention or motive for purchasing and disposing of the dwelling-house and making a gain. That being the case, if a dwelling-house is acquired by way of a gift, inheritance or benefit from a trust, a restriction pursuant to s. 224(3) is unlikely to succeed.

9.4.4 Expenditure incurred for the purpose of realising a gain (second limb of s. 224(3))

The second limb of s. 224(3) also restricts, albeit partly, the relief available on a disposal of a dwelling-house if there is expenditure incurred after the beginning of the ownership period and it was incurred wholly or partly for the purpose of realising a gain. The effect of this restriction is slightly less stringent than the first limb in that it restricts any gain that is directly attributable to the incurred expenditure only. Examples of such expenditure would be the costs of applying for planning permission or the costs of a release from a restrictive covenant, although strictly speaking any type of expenditure which contributes to the dwelling-house fetching a higher sale price could fall within the terms of the restriction. In practice, HMRC do not restrict main residence relief on expenditure incurred on obtaining planning permission or dealing with restrictive covenants.

160

For obvious reasons, the quantification of expenditure and the gain attributable to it is a specialised task and HMRC seek the help of the Valuation Office Agency for comparison values between the gain that has accrued and the gain that would have accrued without the expenditure.

The marriage value of a dwelling-house

In practice, HMRC officers are instructed to challenge situations where the owner of a leasehold interest in a property acquires the superior interest or freehold of the property. An acquisition of a superior interest may occur at a statutorily-determined price which is below market value and shortly before a full disposal of the entire title. The combined market value of the leasehold and freehold interests may be greater than the separately owned interests and this value is known as the "marriage value".

If an individual who has occupied a dwelling-house as his main residence acquires the freehold interest before a disposal in order to realise the marriage value, the restriction on expenditure incurred for the purpose of realising a gain is likely to come into play. In this situation, the part of the gain attributable to the incurred expenditure will be, in effect, the marriage value of the two interests. The entire marriage value would be the part excluded from main residence relief.

Expenditure by an association of leaseholders which acquires the freehold or superior interest (a longer leasehold for instance) in a jointly occupied building through a vehicle (usually a limited company)[2] may also be caught by the second limb of s. 224(3) if the acquisition occurs *shortly* before a disposal of the enhanced interest. It would be very difficult to argue that the expenditure incurred on such acquisition was not for the purpose of realising a much higher gain. On the other hand, if a leaseholder has cogent evidence to show that an intention to realise a gain was not present when the acquisition of the freehold took place, he may benefit from unrestricted main residence relief.

This situation is better illustrated by HMRC's example at CG 65257:

---

[2] Pursuant to the *Leasehold Reform Housing and Urban Development Act* 1993.

HMRC example

In January 2004 an individual acquires a 99 year lease of a dwelling-house with 63 years of the lease remaining, at a cost of £60,000. He uses the dwelling-house as his only residence. In 2013 he decides to sell the house. To increase its value he acquires the freehold for a payment of £40,000 in February 2013. The house is sold in March 2014 for £250,000. The Valuation Office Agency agrees that if the leasehold interest had been sold in March 2014 it would have fetched £160,000.

The part of the gain which is excluded from relief because of the application of TCGA92/S224 (3) is computed as follows.

	Total Gain	Exempt Gain	Non-exempt gain
	£	£	£
1) Disposal proceeds	250,000		
2) Value of leasehold interest		160,000	
Consideration resulting from acquisition of freehold (1)-(2)			90,000
less Cost of leasehold	60,000	60,000	
less Cost of freehold	40,000		40,000
Gain	**150,000**	**100,000**	**50,000**

The chargeable gain is £50,000 subject to annual exempt amount.

Law: TCGA 1992, s. 224(3)
Guidance: CG 65257

Conversion of a dwelling-house into flats

In the year 2018, with Brexit under way and in an uncertain property market, it is not uncommon to see property owners dividing large dwelling-houses into smaller units and selling them off individually for a large capital gain. In some cases, the owner of the dwelling-house may dispose of all of the new individual flats but in other cases, he may continue to occupy one flat as his main residence whilst disposing of the rest.

In both cases, the disposal of the flats (as parts of the main residence) will be eligible for main residence relief if the individual occupied the original dwelling-house as his main residence throughout the ownership period (or with adjustments for absences, business use, etc.). In a similar vein, if any of the new units are rented before an eventual disposal, some of the gain may be eligible for lettings relief (see **Chapter 6** above).

If the original dwelling-house was occupied by tenants before the conversion, the valuation of the undivided house should take into account those tenancies. If a tenant is given compensation or a payment to ensure swift repossession of the property, the amount paid out could in itself amount to expenditure incurred for the purpose of realising a capital gain and the restriction in the second limb of s. 224(3) would be likely to apply. HMRC usually compute the capital gain by looking at the estimated value of the dwelling-house in its "unconverted" state and any excess of the sale proceeds over that estimated value becomes the "realised" gain and therefore the taxable gain.

10. Disposals in connection with divorce and dissolution of civil partnerships

10.1 Married couples and civil partners

The general rule in TCGA 1992, s. 222(6) is that a married couple or civil partnership may have only one residence between them for the purposes of main residence relief and may make a single joint election only. For the exact statutory wording and a discussion of the implications of this rule see **8.5** above.

In terms of "the period of ownership" within TCGA 1992, s. 223 to 226, in the case of an individual living with his spouse or civil partner, any transfers between spouses or civil partners will not restart the period of ownership. The partner receiving the dwelling-house is treated as starting his ownership at the beginning of the transferor's original period of ownership. The rule applies both to lifetime transfers and also to transfers on death of one of the partners.

It is not all bad news as this rule applies only in cases where the transfer occurs when the dwelling-house (or part of it) is in fact the only or main residence of the couple. This means that in other transfers of dwelling-houses between spouses, the ownership period will be reset in the usual way.

This rule has the peculiar possibility of being advantageous or disadvantageous for married couples or civil partners depending on the facts of a particular case.

Example

Chris and Teri get married in 2010 and start to live together in a dwelling-house which Teri inherited in 1995. As a wedding present Teri gifts half of the freehold of the house to Chris and they agree that they will carry out minor repairs before selling it in 2015. Chris will be taxable on his interest in half of the freehold on any sale but by virtue of s. 222(7)(a), he is deemed to have owned his interest since 1995. Teri's occupation of the house as her only residence will be also regarded as Chris' occupation throughout the period of ownership. This means that although Chris was absent from the dwelling-house from 1995 to 2010, he will benefit from full main residence relief on the entire capital gain realised from his share of the freehold.

The position would be different if Teri had not occupied the inherited house for much of the period of ownership (because she had another residence). If, once Teri marries Chris, they both elect the inherited dwelling-house as their main residence and if they decide to sell it, any transfer of the dwelling-house during a period when the couple are not occupying it as a main residence, will be done as a no gain/ no loss transfer and the period of ownership will restart for Chris upon the date of the transfer. This means that any periods of absence by Teri can be "washed out" by the transfer.

Law: TCGA 1992, s. 222(6), (7)(a)

10.2 Breakdown of marriage or civil partnership

10.2.1 Consequences of separation

The tax treatment of a main residence occupied by a married couple or civil partners outlined at **10.1** above applies as long as the couple lives together. This is a natural reading of section 222(6) which refers to "an individual living with his spouse or civil partner". There is no definition or guidance as to what "living together" means but in the author's view, it is prudent to think of it as "living together" in an interpersonal relationship and as a couple. If, in fact, it transpires that the couple occupied the same dwelling-house but were separated and not living as a couple, it would be difficult to show that they were "living together" for the purposes of main residence relief.

For the purposes of main residence relief, if a marriage or civil partnership breaks down and the couple separates, the following consequences will ensue:

- An election made jointly pursuant to section 222(6)(a) will cease to have effect for the spouse or partner who moves out of the marital home ("the parting partner") and would become obsolete for the remaining partner as that person would in fact be occupying the dwelling-house as his or her only or main residence;

- Each partner would be considered an individual again for the purposes of main residence relief and would be

> entitled to elect another dwelling-house as a main residence;
>
> • If a joint election is in place and the partner occupying the marital home as his actual main residence owns another dwelling-house, that individual should consider writing to HMRC to displace the election and if appropriate elect another residence as his main residence;
>
> • The parting partner should also consider whether an election in respect of another dwelling-house would be appropriate. In some cases, such an election may hinder main residence relief if the parting partner sells or transfers his interest in the marital home to his ex-partner (see **10.3** below).

10.2.2   *Temporary separations*

Cases where there has been a short-term or long-term separation with one of the partners owning and occupying an interim residence should be approached with caution. If a spouse or civil partner sells a dwelling-house which was occupied during a temporary separation, HMRC would normally treat any capital gain which accrues as not being eligible for main residence relief. This is on the basis that occupation must be of a permanent nature and that if there is a reconciliation on the cards, any interim accommodation simply amounts to a stop gap measure and not a residence. In those cases, evidence of the status of the relationship at the time may be essential to prove that the separation was envisaged as permanent even though it subsequently transpired to be only temporary. The couple should be able to show an intention to part permanently, perhaps in the form of broken communication, change of address for correspondence, change of General Practitioner and other services, etc.

This point may be illustrated by three recent cases.

Benford

In *Benford v HMRC,* the taxpayer bought a three-bedroom property in his sole name in March 2005 for £124,500 and sold it in September 2005 for £175,000, realising a capital gain. Mr Benford was married throughout the period of ownership of the second property and argued that he had occupied it as his only residence

166

during a period of separation from his wife which happened to coincide with the period of ownership. During oral evidence given under oath, he explained to the First-tier Tribunal that:

> "There were no carpets or rugs just plain wooden floor boards, no heating, no cooking or food storage facilities, no furniture to speak of and nowhere to hang his clothes which he stored on the floor. Mr Benford told us that he slept on an inflatable bed and that he had a kettle and bought takeaway food. He said that he also had meals and showers at both the matrimonial home where Mrs Benford still lived and at his mother's house which was "10 minutes away" which was also where he took his washing."

The taxpayer had continued to receive all correspondence in the marital home and two monthly electricity bills provided for the second property amounted to £9.48 and £11.86 respectively. The local Council had confirmed to HMRC that the taxpayer had not paid council tax on the property as it had been "uninhabitable" during the six-month period.

The evidence and terms of the separation from his wife were sketchy and he could not provide exact dates to the Tribunal. The taxpayer told the Tribunal that the marriage had failed towards the end of 2004, that they had spent that Christmas together for the sake of their children and that he had started looking for a place to live soon afterwards. Mr Benford was not assisted by the fact that his youngest son was conceived during the alleged period of separation. The Tribunal found that whilst the taxpayer had occupied the dwelling-house during the ownership period, the occupation did not have the permanence and degree of continuity necessary to make it a main residence.

Case: *Benford v HMRC* [2011] UKFTT 457 (TC)

Clarke

In *Clarke v HMRC,* the taxpayer had to buy a property located along a direct route between his matrimonial home and his children's school due to the separation from his wife, who was having an affair and who was suffering from mental health issues (including more than one suicide attempt). At first, Mr Clarke bought the dwelling-house with the help of a three-day business loan and had "begged

167

and borrowed" furniture in order to enable his children to stay with him two to three times a week away from the emotional distress caused by their mother. After four months of living in the house, the appellant obtained planning permission to build another house in the house's grounds. He therefore sold the main house, moved in with his mother and started the building project himself. He lived in a different room of the house whilst the rest of the house was being built.

After a suicide attempt by his estranged wife, Mr Clarke felt he had no choice but to move back into the marital home in order to care for and protect his children. He put his new property on the market and sold it four months later. The marital home was eventually sold when his ex-wife moved out with her new partner, and the taxpayer then moved to another converted house with his children. The taxpayer claimed main residence relief on the sales of the second home and the newly built one.

The taxpayer presented statements from family and friends as well as a report from his ex-wife's psychologist confirming the fragile state she had been in. The Tribunal found Mr Clarke and his story entirely credible and allowed his appeal.

Case: *Clarke v HMRC* [2011] UKFTT 619 (TC)

Bradley

Third, and as already mentioned in **2.3.5** above, Mrs Susan Bradley in *Bradley v HMRC* was at all relevant times married to Mr Bradley and lived in a property jointly owned with him until August 2007. Mrs Bradley also owned a semi-detached house and a small "bedsit" flat, both of which were let to tenants.

Prior to August 2007, the relationship between the Bradleys had taken a turn for the worse and this led to Mrs Bradley moving out of the marital home and into her small flat which at the time was conveniently vacant. When the tenancy at her other house expired in April 2008 she moved there. When she first moved, the house was in a poor decorative state and Mrs Bradley repainted it, repaired the kitchen and bought new appliances and fittings to make it more of a "home". Mrs Bradley explained in evidence that her intention was to separate permanently from her husband and obtain a divorce. To this end, she visited solicitors specialising in family law to clarify her rights but did not file divorce papers. Mrs Bradley supported herself and continued to visit the marital home to see her youngest daughter and to collect her post which she still received there. She was suffering from depression at this stage and was undergoing treatment. She told the Tribunal that she had not been functioning well at this time and therefore had not had the presence of mind to change her address on her bank accounts or utilities. She did have proof of council tax payments for both her small flat and the semi-detached house.

Despite the alleged intention to separate permanently from her husband, there was evidence of an instruction dated 20 March 2008 from Mrs Bradley to local estate agents to place the semi-detached house she was then occupying on the market. The market was poor due to the economic downturn and there were no offers from buyers. The house stayed on the market throughout Mrs Bradley's period of occupation.

The Bradleys eventually reconciled and Mrs Bradley moved back to the marital home in November 2008. Mrs Bradley's semi-detached property was then sold in January 2009.

The Tribunal decided that they were satisfied that when Mrs Bradley had left the marital home in August 2007, her intention was to separate permanently from her husband and to divorce him after two years' separation. However, the Tribunal recognised that this fact in itself did not mean that Mrs Bradley's second house qualified for main residence relief. They had to explore whether Mrs Bradley had occupied the property as her only or main residence.

Due to the fact that even before Mrs Bradley had moved into her second property, she had already placed it on the market and her instructions were still in place when she reconciled with her husband, the Tribunal found that "she never intended to live permanently [there], it was only ever going to be a temporary home, and therefore it was never her residence". The Tribunal drew support for this finding from *Goodwin* and the First-tier Tribunal's decision in *Metcalf*. It is important to note that in Goodwin, the taxpayer placed his farmhouse on the market because three days after he moved into it he completed a purchase of another house which he treated as his residence for the following tax year. In other words, he could not have intended to live at the farmhouse if he had

169

already decided to reside permanently elsewhere. That was certainly not the case for Mrs Bradley and perhaps too much reliance was placed on the very different *Goodwin* facts by the Tribunal in this case.

Indeed, if one compares the decision in *Piers Moore* (see **2.3.6** above) to *Bradley*, the reasoning of the FTT is very hard to reconcile. In *Moore* the taxpayer moved out of the marital home in 2006 because his long-term marriage was in difficulties. He moved into a buy-to-let flat he had owned for a number of years after a tenant who did not keep up with rent payments had moved out. He had taken all his clothes and some furniture to the flat, and the rest of the furniture had been purchased. In March or April 2007, Mr Moore had started a romantic relationship with another woman and around the same time, the flat had been put on the market for sale.

Mr Moore's girlfriend (who subsequently became his wife) also put her own house on the market in May 2007. They eventually moved into a jointly owned home. Mr Moore did not return to his ex-wife and the FTT accepted that there was no realistic chance of reconciliation. The FTT, however, found that his occupation of the flat did not have the sufficient permanence and continuity to amount to a occupation as a residence. The Tribunal came to this conclusion because Mr Moore had organised his financial affairs in early 2007 for an impending purchase and because shortly after he moved to the flat, he had a "serious hope" or expectation that he would move out with his new partner.

Taking into account that Mr Moore did not reconcile with his ex-wife and had lived in his flat "not less than 3 months, and perhaps as much as 5 months before it began to be marketed" and almost eight months before its sale completed, it difficult to see why the FTT did not find sufficient permanence or continuity. This case seemed to be some way away from the facts in *Goodwin* and *Bradley*.

Cases: *Bradley v HMRC* [2013] UKFTT 131 (TC); *Moore v HMRC* [2013] UKFTT 433 (TC)

10.3 Divorce and dissolution of civil partnership

In practice, a final divorce or *decree absolute* has no impact on main residence relief as this is – under normal circumstances – an official confirmation of the couple no longer "living together". The term "normal circumstances" recognises that there could be a minority of cases where the couple continue to "live together" until the final divorce or in exceptional circumstances decide to continue living together in the same dwelling-house despite a divorce and without formally separating.

When dealing with the tax consequences of a divorce, it is important in the first instance to consider who the beneficial owners of the property are and what equitable interest each partner has in the joint marital home. The legal owner of the residence is not necessarily the sole beneficial owner and he or she may be holding part of the residence in trust for the other partner. A spouse or civil partner who is not an owner of the legal title of the joint residence will still have an equitable interest in the property directly proportional to any contributions made in money or money's worth.

The extent of the equitable interest of each partner upon divorce is important because on a disposal of the residence, the capital gain of each partner will amount to the net gain on a transfer of the property divided between them in the ratio of their respective equitable interests. This division will happen irrespective of who incurred the expenditure in the first instance. Main or only residence relief is then calculated taking into account the joint period of ownership and occupation as a main residence up to the date when they ceased living together (if earlier than the final divorce) and the final 18 months of the period of ownership.

A difficulty arises where a spouse or civil partner moves out of the joint main residence on separation or divorce and transfers his or her interest in the dwelling-house to the other spouse or partner as part of a financial agreement. Under a strict reading of the statutory provisions, the transferor could not benefit from main residence relief for the period after he moved out of the residence (except for the last 18 months of ownership).

Former Extra-Statutory Concession D6 was enacted as TCGA 1992, s. 225B with effect from 6 April 2009 and the provision ensures that the parting partner benefits from relief as if he had continued to live in the dwelling-house as follows:

(1) Where an individual—

(a) **ceases to live with his spouse or civil partner** in a dwelling-house or part of a dwelling-house which is their only or main residence, **and**

(b) subsequently disposes of, or of an interest in, the dwelling-house or part to the spouse or civil partner,

then, if conditions A to C are met, **sections 222 to 224 shall apply as if the dwelling-house** or part **continued to be** the individual's only or **main residence** until the disposal.

Five conditions must be satisfied in order to benefit fully from the terms of s. 225B:

(i) the parting partner ceases to live in a dwelling-house which was their only or main residence;

(ii) the parting partner subsequently disposes of, or of an interest in, the dwelling-house or part of the dwelling-house to his former partner – not a third party;

(iii) the said disposal is a result of:

- an agreement between the parties made in contemplation of divorce or dissolution of a civil partnership; or

- a court order confirming a divorce, dissolution or annulment;

(iv) in the interim period between the parting partner ceasing to live in the dwelling-house and disposing of his interest to his former partner, the remaining partner has occupied the same dwelling-house as his or her main residence;

(v) the parting partner has not given an election notice in respect of any other residence for any part of the interim period.

Finally, in order to benefit from the computational rules in TCGA 1992, s. 223, a claim must be made (s. 225B(5)).

The end result of s. 225B is that the transferor spouse or civil partner is able to treat the dwelling-house or part of the dwelling-house as his only or main residence for an unlimited period of time between moving out and transferring his interest to his former spouse or partner.

Divorce and dissolution are often hostile events and it is important to ensure that the remaining partner understands and agrees that he or she *must* remain in the dwelling-house and occupy it as his or her main residence until the time of any transfer as relief may otherwise be irreversibly lost.

Law: TCGA 1992, s. 225B

Guidance: CG 65300-65356

10.4 Mesher orders

Following the case of *Mesher v Mesher and Hall*, and taking account of the statutory duty of care in respect of the interests of any minor children upon divorce, the Court may make a *Mesher* order which directs that the marital home should be retained by both spouses or civil partners in their joint names on trust and that (usually) the mother should remain in occupation until the children reach a specified age (normally 18 years old). Other *Mesher* orders may compel a spouse or civil partner to retain his or her interest in the marital house on trust for a limited period until, for instance, the other partner remarries, re-enters a civil partnership or dies.

In other cases parties may come to a contractual agreement on similar terms to a *Mesher* order but avoiding a Court order with the associated delay and legal costs.

HMRC treat such orders as creating a settlement for the purposes of CGT and main residence relief. This means that the party holding the interest in the marital dwelling-house is transferring that interest into a trust for the benefit of his or her children or former partner. As a result, the trust property (i.e. the marital residence) is eligible for main residence relief under the terms of TCGA 1992, s. 225 as long as it is occupied as a main residence by the remaining spouse or partner who is entitled to live there as part of a *Mesher* order or agreement. This means that any disposal of the residence would be eligible for main residence relief in the period between separation and eventual sale or other disposal, without adversely affecting the parting partner's eligibility for main residence relief on another residence subsequently acquired.

Whenever the specified period in the *Mesher* order or binding agreement comes to an end, the trust settlement will similarly come to an end and the former spouses or civil partners will become absolutely entitled to the dwelling-house. This event will be deemed to be a disposal at current market value as trustees (under TCGA 1992, s. 71).

HMRC illustrate the tax treatment of *Mesher* orders with the following example:

HMRC example

Mr C bought a house in 2000 and occupied it with his wife as their only residence until 2004, when they separated. Mr C moved into rented accommodation while Mrs C continued to reside in the house. They divorced in March 2008. By a Court Order in May 2008 Mr C was ordered to hold the property on trust for Mrs C and the children until the youngest child, who was then 14, was 18. The youngest child reached 18 in January 2012 and the property was sold in February 2012.

The Court Order in May 2008 results in a transfer into trust and so is an occasion of charge on Mr C under TCGA92/S70. Mr C makes a claim for TCGA92/S225B to apply and so private residence relief will be due in full.

There is a second occasion of charge on Mr C in January 2012 when the youngest child reaches 18. You should allow full relief under TCGA92/S225, see CG65400+. No relief is due when the dwelling-house is sold in February 2012 but any increase in value between January and February is likely to be negligible and so a chargeable gain is unlikely to accrue.

Whilst the example above has Mr C moving into rented accommodation after separation, if he were to acquire a second residence in the interim period, the effect of the *Mesher* order on the eligibility for main residence relief on the marital home would be exactly the same.

Finally, it should be borne in mind that with the changes to inheritance tax introduced in 2006, a *Mesher* order would mean that the marital home is "relevant property" in the settlement. There may then be an immediate IHT charge if the residence exceeds the inheritance tax threshold and a potential 10-year anniversary charge if the trust is intended to last longer than ten years.

Law: TCGA 1992, s. 71, 225

Case: *Mesher v Mesher and Hall* [1980] 1 All ER 126

11. Trusts, settlements and personal representatives

11.1 Residence occupied under the terms of a settlement

11.1.1 Introduction

TCGA 1992, s. 225 provides that main residence relief[1] is also available on any gain accruing to trustees on the disposal of "settled property being an asset within section 222(1)" where the dwelling-house (or part) has been the only or main residence of a beneficiary entitled to occupy it under the terms of the settlement. The period of occupation of the beneficiary and the ownership period must coincide, otherwise any relief would be restricted to the period of occupation only.

11.1.2 Settled property

Settled property is defined by TCGA 1992, s. 68 as "any property held in trust" excluding property held by a person as nominee for another person or as a bare trustee.

Recent case on "settled property"

In *Wagstaff v HMRC*, the First-tier Tribunal had to determine whether main residence relief (pursuant to s. 225) was available on the disposal of a flat occupied by the mother of one of the taxpayers under a mutual agreement which allowed her to occupy it for life or until remarriage.

The said flat was purchased by the taxpayer's mother in 1990. Six years later, she transferred the flat to the taxpayer, her son, and his wife for £45,000 pursuant to a short written agreement. The agreement provided that the mother was entitled to continue living at the flat for free for the remainder of her life or until remarriage subject to a one-off payment of £5,000. The mother continued to occupy the flat until 2005 when she became unable to use stairs by reason of a knee-replacement surgery. She moved in with the taxpayers until a replacement single-storey home was found in June

---

[1] Including the rules on amount and computation of relief, permitted area, grounds and gardens, period of ownership, allowable absences, lettings relief and restrictions.

176

2006. The original flat remained unoccupied until that date but it still held her furniture and personal belongings until it was sold, with her agreement, to a third party in March 2007.

HMRC argued that the agreement between the parties amounted to a "lease for life" that did not affect the taxpayers' absolute right to dispose of the flat and that did not amount to a trust. Accordingly, the taxpayers were said not to be trustees and the flat not settled property for the purposes of TCGA 1992, s. 225.

The FTT held that HMRC's approach raised the fundamental question of the nature of the mother's rights under the arrangement with the taxpayers and how those rights "impacted" on the taxpayers' interest in the flat. Essentially, what had to be decided was whether or not the taxpayers were "absolutely entitled" to their interest in the flat with no restrictions and, if not, whether those restrictions were a matter of trust or contract.

The Tribunal concluded that the arrangement did not contain the formal language expected of a grant of a lease for life or the usual terms used under a lease. Further, there was no guarantee of exclusive occupation by the mother and at best she held a contractual licence. Nevertheless, the agreement cemented contractual obligations between the parties and these obligations extended to the taxpayers owning the flat but not being free to dispose of it without the approval of their mother. This was, for all intents and purposes, a trust relationship and the taxpayers' interest in the flat therefore amounted to "settled property". The appeal was decided in favour of the taxpayers.

Law: TCGA 1992, s. 68, 225

Case: *Veronica and Stephen Wagstaff v HMRC* [2014] UKFTT 43 (TC)

11.1.3   An asset within TCGA 1992, s. 222(1)

The wording chosen by the draftsman in s. 225 indicates that the extension of main residence relief to trustees is intended to be widely construed. This means that trustees may claim main residence relief on the disposal of a wide range of assets including a traditional dwelling-house or part thereof as well as a legal or equitable interest in a dwelling-house. In addition, the relief will extend to a separate disposal of land which has been occupied and used for the enjoyment of the dwelling-house as gardens and grounds (subject to any permitted area restrictions and reasonable enjoyment arguments).

Law: TCGA 1992, s. 222(1), 225

11.1.4   *Entitlement to occupy under the terms of settlement*

Legal right

A beneficiary of a trust of land who has an interest in possession in the land is given an automatic right to occupy the land by the *Trusts of Land and Appointments of Trustees Act* 1996, s. 12. This means that as long as the purpose of the trust includes making the land (and buildings) available for the beneficiary's occupation, and it is in fact available and suitable for occupation, this will amount to an "entitlement to occupy" under the terms of the trust. It should be noted that it is generally recognised that the trust deed must permit the occupation by the beneficiary as opposed to a case where the trustees allow someone to occupy the dwelling-house for no consideration without an express power to do so. Conversely, the payment of rent in itself does not prevent a beneficiary from being entitled to occupy the dwelling-house and, in some cases, rent may be charged on the occupying beneficiary so as to implement fair treatment for all beneficiaries who may also be entitled to occupy the residence.

Discretionary right

In terms of discretionary trusts, in *Sansom v Peay* the High Court held that the relief under s. 225 extended to discretionary trustees too. In that case the trustees of a discretionary settlement acquired a dwelling-house for the occupation of certain beneficiaries in 1966. The trust deed contained a clause which empowered the trustees to permit any beneficiary to reside in a dwelling-house subject to the trust on such conditions as to the rent (or other matters) as the trustees in their discretion saw fit. Certain beneficiaries under the trust occupied the dwelling-house as their main residence throughout the trustees' period of ownership until its disposal in 1971. The Revenue raised a CGT assessment on the gain accrued on the disposal arguing that "a person entitled to occupy it under the terms of the settlement" meant strictly a person who, under the terms of the settlement, always had during the relevant period a right to occupy and to remain in occupation. They further argued that the beneficiaries did not have an absolute right of occupation and were mere licensees of the trustees under a revocable agreement.

The trustees appealed the assessment to the General Commissioners who dismissed the appeal. On an appeal by way of case stated, the question for the High Court (Brightman J) was whether or not the beneficiaries of the discretionary trust were "entitled to occupy [the dwelling-house] under the terms of the settlement". The Court held that FA 1965, s. 29(9)[2] was capable of bearing both a broad and a strict construction but that following the intention of Parliament when enacting the provision (i.e. to exempt from liability to CGT the proceeds of sale of a person's home in light of the "evil of inflation"), the words of the section permitted a broader construction.

In that case, as certain beneficiaries were in occupation pursuant to the exercise by the Trustees of their discretionary powers under the trust deed which permitted them to occupy and to remain in occupation until such time as permission was withdrawn, "looking at the matter at the date of disposal, the beneficiaries were persons who, in the events which happened, were entitled to occupy the house and did occupy it under the terms of the settlement".

Tenants in common

If the trustees of a settlement own a dwelling-house as tenants in common with another person (or persons) who also happens to occupy the house as his only or main residence, the trustees should still be able to claim main residence relief on their share of the interest in the dwelling-house under s. 225. The "entitlement" test is widely drafted and in the author's view covers situations where a beneficiary has a right of occupation as a co-owner of the land as long as the terms of the trust also grant them a separate right to occupation. This is particularly useful in cases where a dwelling-

---

[2] A predecessor of s. 225.

house is co-owned by a couple and one partner's share is held on trust when the partner dies.

Law: FA 1965, s. 29(9); *Trusts of Land and Appointments of Trustees Act 1996*, s. 12; TCGA 1992, s. 225
Case: *Sansom & Another (Ridge Settlement Trustees) v Peay (HMIT)* [1976] 1 WLR 1073; (1976) 52 TC 1

11.1.5   Who should have ownership of the dwelling-house?

Pursuant to s. 225A, the rules and provisions contained in TCGA 1992, s. 222 to 224 apply as if all references to an individual should read as "trustees".

As a consequence, questions of ownership, amount and apportionment of relief and period of ownership should always be answered by reference to the trustees of the settlement and not to the beneficiaries or anyone else related to the trustees. It should be noted, however, that trustees who have joint ownership as tenants in common should also be eligible for the exemption as long as the other conditions in s. 225 are met (see **11.1.4** above).

11.1.6 Occupation of the dwelling-house

As outlined in **11.1.5,** s. 225 applies the main residence relief rules in s. 222 to 224 as if the references to an "individual" should be substituted for "trustees". This substitution does not extend to the occupation of the dwelling-house. Any enquiry about qualifying occupation should relate to the beneficiary of the settlement only. Following the decision by Brightman J in *Sansom v Peay,* occupation under the terms of the settlement should be considered at the date of the disposal (see **11.1.4** above).

The beneficiary is required to occupy the settled property throughout the trustees' period of ownership. Looking at the application of s. 222 to 223 in the first part of s. 225, it appears that the provisions on the last 18 months of ownership and periods of absence must be applied to the person entitled to occupy as if he or she were the 'individual' owner of the dwelling-house.

The position is not entirely clear when there are multiple beneficiaries entitled to occupy the dwelling-house under the terms of a settlement and they occupy the dwelling-house at different but consecutive times.

Example

The Generous Trust owns a two-bedroom flat and holds no other property. A specific clause of the trust deed grants interests in the flat to two sisters as follows: to Meredith for life and then to Christina for life with the remainder going to Christina's infant child. Meredith moves in straightaway and occupies the flat as her main residence for five years until she joins the Royal Navy and is deployed to a foreign country. The flat remains unoccupied for four years whilst she remains absent due to her duties abroad. Meredith is killed in action. Christina (together with her son) moves into the flat soon after Meredith's death and continues to occupy it as her only residence.

Under the rules in s. 223(3)(b), Meredith's absence of four years is a period of absence which would be treated as a period of occupation if there was occupation as a main residence for the periods straddling the absence. Strictly speaking, Meredith's death means that she is unable to meet the requirements of Condition B in s. 223(3B) and occupy the flat once again after her absence. However, the relevant test is "that after the period [of absence] ...there was a time when the dwelling-house was the individual's only or main residence". According to s. 225 the reference to "individual" should be substituted for "a person entitled to occupy [the dwelling-house] under the terms of the settlement". That being the case, in the author's view, as Christina is a person entitled to occupy the flat under the trust deed, she can step into the shoes of the "individual" in s. 223(3B) and fulfil the requirement of occupation after Meredith's period of absence.

Law: TCGA 1992, s. 223(3)(b), (3B), s. 225
Case: *Sansom & Another (Ridge Settlement Trustees) v Peay (HMIT)* [1976] 1 WLR 1073; (1976) 52 TC 1

11.1.7 Restrictions on user

In a similar vein, if the beneficiary occupies the property (or part of it) exclusively for business or trade use, a restriction on relief or adjustment of relief under s. 224 should take effect for the trustees. Section 224 does not distinguish between business use by the owner and business use by the occupier.

Law: TCGA 1992, s. 224

11.2 Specific rules for claiming main residence relief under section 225

Similar to the rules under s. 222(6)(a) (joint election for married couples and civil partners) where a beneficiary (who is entitled to occupy the dwelling-house under the terms of a settlement) occupies a settled property as his only or main residence, but owns or has a legal interest in another residence, a notice under s. 222(5)(a) electing the settled property as his main residence must be a joint notice with the trustees.

One significant difference between main residence relief available for individuals and for trustees is the requirement for trustees to make a claim for the relief on any disposal of a relevant residence. If a claim is not made, main residence relief will not be secured.

Law: TCGA 1992, s. 222(5)(a), 222(6)(a), 225

11.3 Interaction with lettings relief

The express terms of s. 225 require that in order for a claim for main residence relief by trustees to be successful there must be both ownership of the dwelling-house and occupation of it by a person entitled to occupy it during the period of ownership. If the trustees own a settled property and let it out to a third person, the second element of s. 225 (i.e. occupation by a beneficiary) is unfulfilled and relief will not be due. In (unusual) situations where a beneficiary is in occupation of part of a dwelling-house and the other part is let to a third party, the trustees could benefit from:

- full main residence relief on the gain accrued on the part of the dwelling-house occupied by the beneficiary; and
- lettings relief on the part of the gain which would be chargeable by reason of the third-party letting, up to the maximum of £40,000.

11.4 Main residence held by personal representatives

Section 225A of TCGA 1992 (introduced by FA 2004 to codify former Extra-Statutory Concession D5) provides that main residence relief is also available for personal representatives administering the estate of a deceased person, on a disposal of a dwelling-house or part thereof or a relevant interest in a dwelling-house, as long as the following conditions are satisfied:

(i)   Both before and after the deceased's death, the dwelling-house (or part) was the only or main residence of one or more individuals; and

(ii)   One of the individuals (or two or more individuals) occupying the dwelling-house as a main residence is entitled under a will or under the rules of intestacy to the whole or part of at least 75% of the net proceeds of disposal (absolutely or for life).

This means that where two or more individuals occupied the property as their only or main residence at the relevant time, the 75% condition is tested by accumulating the separate interests of all the individuals concerned: it is not necessary for all the individuals in question to have such an interest for the condition to be met.

For these purposes the term "net proceeds of disposal" means:

- the sale proceeds realised by the personal representatives; *less*

- any incidental costs allowable under TCGA 1992, s. 38(1)(c); *but*

- assuming that none of the proceeds will be required by the personal representatives to cover the liabilities of the deceased's estate including IHT.

Similarly to the occupation of a dwelling-house by a beneficiary under the terms of a trust, main residence relief rules contained in sections 222 to 224 apply as if the references to "individual" read "personal representatives" except when occupation of the dwelling-house comes into question.

The relief under s. 225A is not automatic and a claim must be made by the personal representatives in accordance with procedural requirements and time limits in TMA 1970.

Any notice electing for the deceased's dwelling-house to be treated as a main residence should be made jointly by the personal representatives administering the estate and by the individual(s) entitled to occupy it under the will or intestacy rules.

In practice, in situations where two or more individuals are entitled to occupy the dwelling-house (or part of it), but only one occupies the house as a main residence (and is therefore entitled to the exemption), only the proportion of the gain relating to that individual's entitlement would be eligible for main residence relief. A way round this loss of relief would be (subject to a valuation of the dwelling and the deceased's estate) for the personal representatives to allocate the individual's share of the legal title or interest in the house so that he may claim individual's main residence relief on his part of the gain.

Law: TCGA 1992, s. 225A; FA 2004, Sch. 22, para. 5

11.5 Interaction with cases where gift relief was obtained under TCGA 1992, s. 260 and exception

11.5.1 Policy objective of the rules

For disposals made on or after 10 December 2003, FA 2004 also introduced new measures (TCGA 1992, s. 226A and 226B) which were intended to "counter tax avoidance schemes which are designed to secure that gains arising on the disposal of other properties are able to benefit from private residence relief".

In reality these measures go further; they prevent any planning arrangements whereby capital gains realised on second homes (i.e. not main residences) are washed out by gifts to connected persons (for instance children) who could then live in and occupy the dwelling-house as their only or main residence.

11.5.2 Gift relief or main residence relief but not both

Thus, relief is denied to individuals, or to trustees of a settlement, where they acquire a dwelling-house in a transaction in respect of which "gift" relief was elected or claimed under TCGA 1992, s. 260.

In essence, s. 226A has retrospective effect as it applies to any disposal on or after 10 December 2003 (and it applies to gains held over and also any further gain accruing after the date on which the transfer originating the held over gain was made). However, if the claim for holdover relief was in respect of a gain accrued before that date, transitional provisions in FA 2004 will apply (but only where the original disposal took place before that date) and main residence relief continues to be available in respect of the period of ownership before 10 December 2003 in a time-apportioned fraction.

If the property is considered a "business asset", holdover relief may be claimed under TCGA 1992, s. 165. This type of held over gain is not affected by the restrictions in s. 226A.

In the event that a main residence relief claim is more favourable than a gift relief claim previously made, s. 226A(6) provides the opportunity to treat a revoked claim for gift relief as never having been made.

Law: TCGA 1992, s. 165, 226A, 260; FA 2004, Sch. 22, para. 8

11.5.3 Exception to s. 226A – maintenance funds for historic buildings

TCGA 1992, s. 226B provides that the restriction on main residence relief in situations where gift relief has previously been claimed is subject to one exception. If the trustees of a settlement make an election pursuant to ITA 2007, s. 508 (trustees' election in respect of income arising from heritage maintenance property) then the restrictions of s. 226A are disapplied. This exception applies to a settlement or any part of a settlement and in relation to each year of assessment in which a claim for gift relief is made.

Law: TCGA 1992, s. 226B; ITA 2007, s. 508

12. Main residence of dependent relative before 6 April 1988

12.1 Application

An individual (or married couples or civil partners living together) may also claim exemption in respect of a capital gain accruing on the disposal of, or of an interest in, a single dwelling-house or part of a dwelling-house which, on 5 April 1988 or at any earlier time in their period of ownership, was the sole residence of his dependent relative.

If the individual eligible for main residence relief so claims, he may benefit from relief on the disposal of such a dwelling-house, together with its grounds and gardens pursuant to s. 222 to 224, as if the dwelling-house had in fact been occupied as his main or only residence during the period of residence by the dependent relative.

Finally, if the individual is eligible for main residence relief under TCGA 1992, s. 226, he would also be entitled to relief on the last 18 months of ownership irrespective of whether or not his dependent relative was occupying the dwelling-house.

No new dwelling-houses can qualify for relief under s. 226 as it has historical and transitional application only. This means that dwelling-houses which qualified because of occupation by a dependent relative before 6 April 1988 cannot then qualify for a further period after that date as a result of occupation by a different dependent relative.

Law: TCGA 1992, s. 222-224, 226

12.2 Conditions

12.2.1 Overview

TCGA 1992, s. 226(1) requires an individual (or married couple or civil partners living together) who provides a sole residence for a dependent relative since 6 April 1988 to do so rent-free and without any other consideration throughout the period of occupation. "Sole residence" indicates that there can only be one residence provided to a dependent relative per married couple or civil partnership (s. 226(4)). In addition:

(a)   the dwelling-house must have been acquired before 6 April 1988; and

(b)   at some time since its acquisition and before that date, the dwelling-house must have been occupied as the sole residence of a dependent relative.

For an analysis of some of these conditions, see below.

12.2.2   Rent-free

For relief to apply under this section, the residence provided to a dependent relative must have been provided free of rent or any other consideration. On a strict application of this rule, the requirement for no consideration to exchange between the two parties would mean that any payment whatsoever (even if to cover council tax or small expenses) would disqualify the individual from claiming the exemption. In practice, this strict requirement has been relaxed by way of concession by HMRC. Extra-Statutory Concession D20 provides that:

> "Where relief is claimed under [TCGA 1992, s. 226] in respect of the disposal by an individual of a dwelling house which has at any time been the sole residence of a dependent relative, the condition that the dwelling house must have been provided rent free and without any other consideration will be regarded as satisfied where the dependent relative pays all or part of the occupier's council tax and the cost of repairs to the dwelling house attributable to normal wear and tear. Additionally, the benefit of the relief will not be lost where the dependent relative makes other payments in respect of the property either to the individual or to a third party, provided that no net income is receivable by the individual, taking one year with another. For this purpose net income will be computed in accordance with the normal rules of Schedule A [as it then was], except that any mortgage payments (including both income and capital elements) and any other payments made by the dependent relative as consideration for the provision of the property, whether made directly to the mortgagee or other recipient or indirectly via the individual will be credited as receipts. The deductions to be debited will be computed in accordance with the normal rules of Schedule A."

187

Caution should be exercised in cases where a dwelling-house was transferred to children or grandchildren in order to mitigate inheritance tax liabilities for the parents. The idea is usually that the parents will continue to reside in the dwelling-house and that, on a future disposal, the transferees will be able to claim full exemption from CGT on the basis of s. 226. However, if there is an explicit agreement between the parties that the parents will have an unlimited right to reside in the house in exchange for its legal title, then it will be very difficult to argue that the house was not provided for "any other consideration". Main residence relief may then be lost in its totality for the entire period of occupation.

Guidance: ESC D20

12.2.3   Period of occupation

Section 226(3) restricts the availability of relief in situations where a dwelling-house has been occupied by a dependent relative before the key date of 6 April 1988 but he or she ceases to occupy the dwelling-house or part of it as his or her sole residence before or after this date. Any periods after a dependent relative has ceased to occupy the dwelling-house, or part of it, will be disregarded and will not qualify for the exemption.

A common sense approach should be taken in determining what "ceases ... to be the sole residence" means in practice. Periods of holiday, stays in hospital for short-term treatment or short periods of respite care followed by re-occupation of the dwelling-house are unlikely to constitute ceasing to occupy. Conversely, a long-term absence (even if for medical reasons) followed by sporadic occupation of the dwelling-house is more likely than not to amount to ceasing to occupy as a sole residence starting from the first day of the absence.

In a similar vein, if periods of absence from the residence begin to be longer in duration than actual occupation, this could also constitute ceasing to occupy as a sole residence.

Law: TCGA 1992, s. 222-224, 226

12.3 Definitions

According to s. 226(6), "dependent relative" means, in relation to an individual:

(a)   any relative of his or of his wife who is incapacitated by old age or infirmity from maintaining himself; or

(b)   his or his wife's mother who, whether or not incapacitated, is either widowed, or living apart from her husband, or a single woman in consequence of dissolution or annulment of marriage.

In the first instance, it should be noted that financial dependence is not a requirement of the rules and that, therefore, the relative's income and capital are not relevant considerations to take into account in determining whether or not relief is due.

Although s. 226(7) explains that references in s. 226(6)(a) to "wife" should also be construed as "husband", the antiquated provision does not specify that the relief will be extended to an individual's widowed or lone father. Despite the two categories not being exclusive, the only way in which an individual's father would meet the definition of "dependent relative" would be if he was incapacitated or infirm by advanced age.

There is no definition provided for "relative" so it would be reasonable to assume that anyone who falls within the Oxford dictionary's definition of "a person connected by blood or marriage" would qualify for this relief. HMRC's guidance (at CG 65574) confirms this view and also includes foster, step and adopted relations.

With regards to "old age", there is no definition either. It would be reasonable to argue that anyone over retirement age would qualify as would anyone (regardless of age) who develops a degenerative disease or illness which renders him or her infirm or unable to work or maintain independence.

Law: TCGA 1992, s. 226(6), (7)
Guidance: CG 65574

13. Inheritance tax – residence nil-rate band

13.1 Origin

At Summer Budget 2015, the Chancellor of the Exchequer announced plans to phase in a brand new nil-rate band for transfers of an individual's residence on death. The stated aim of the proposal was as follows:

> "The government recognises that individuals may wish to downsize to a smaller and often less valuable property later in life. Others may have to sell their home for a variety of reasons, for example, because they need to go into residential care. This may mean that they would lose some, or all, of the benefit of the available RNRB. However, the government intends that the new RNRB should not be introduced in such a way as to disincentivise an individual from downsizing or selling their property.
>
> Consequently, the government announced that where part or all of the RNRB might be lost because the deceased had downsized to a less valuable residence or had ceased to own a residence the lost RNRB will still be available – provided that the qualifying conditions were met. The RNRB would apply where the residence is sold (or is no longer owned) on or after 8 July 2015 ..."

Following nine days of public consultation, the proposals were inserted into the draft *Finance Bill (No. 2)* 2015, which went through Parliament with some moderate amendments. Following the Budget announcement and the consultation responses, a number of provisions introduced complex formulas and definitions in order to increase the existing nil-rate band. In other words, the new legislation inserted complex rules into IHTA 1984 for a change which was in itself fairly simple.

13.2 Summary of the provisions and their effect

13.2.1 Overview

Section 8D of IHTA 1984 prescribes that for the purposes of calculating a charge to IHT on a person's death, any value transferred on the disposal of the person's residence will be charged at the rate of 0% as long as:

(a) the person owns a residence, or a share of one, so that it is included in his or her estate (this is not limited to UK property);

(b) the residence has been occupied at some stage by the deceased before death (this is in direct contrast with main residence relief because there is no requirement to have occupied the residence as a main home for a minimum period. However, a buy-to-let property will not qualify);

(c) the deceased's direct descendants inherit the home, or a share of it;

(d) the value transferred does not exceed the "residential enhancement" amount;

(e) the date of death is on or after 6 April 2017; or the person has downsized to a less valuable home or sold, or given away their home after 7 July 2015 (see "Downsizing addition" at **13.2.3** below).

13.2.2   *Phasing in of residential enhancement*

The "residential enhancement" amount will be phased in as follows:

(i) £100,000 for the tax year 2017-18;

(ii) £125,000 for the tax year 2018-19;

(iii) £150,000 for the tax year 2019-20; and

(iv) £175,000 for the tax year 2020-21 and subsequent tax years.

These allocated amounts are available over and above the basic inheritance tax threshold (or nil-rate band) and, after the 2020-21 tax year, the amount will increase in line with the consumer price index.

For estates that are valued at £2m or more, the residence nil-rate band will be tapered away by £1 for every £2 by which the net value exceeds £2m. The value of the residence used for the purposes of the RNRB should be the open market value less any liabilities secured on it (mortgages or loans).

In accordance with new s. 8G of IHTA 1984, if at the time of death there is any unused residence nil-rate, then it can be transferred to the deceased's spouse or civil partner. This is subject to a specific claim for the transfer. The residence nil-rate band may be applied to the whole taxable estate and not just the value of the residence, so the benefit is shared across the whole estate. This provision is generous so that in practice it could mean that the family home which is passed onto, say, the couple's children may end up being exempt for IHT purposes in its entirety. It is, however, important to note that the residence nil-rate band is only available for transfers upon death and not for any lifetime transfers.

Closely inherited

The residence nil-rate band is available when the residence is inherited by a close descendant. For these purposes "inherited" means disposed of by will or the law of intestacy[1] but specifically excludes property that becomes comprised in a trust or settlement on the person's death.

The definition of a "descendant" in new s. 8K is very wide. It includes all lineal descendants like children and grandchildren (including stepchildren, adopted children and foster children) and their spouses or civil partners.

Law: IHTA 1984, s. 8D-8M; F(no.2)A 2015, s. 9

13.2.3 Downsizing addition

FA 2016, s. 93 and Sch. 15 introduced detailed and further provisions dealing with cases where an estate does not qualify for the full amount of residence nil-rate band but where a downsizing addition may be obtained. In essence, if:

- the deceased disposed of a former residence and either downsized to a less valuable residence, or ceased to own a residence, on or after 8 July 2015;
- the former residence would have qualified for the RNRB if it had been kept until death; and
- at least some of the estate is inherited by the deceased's direct descendants,

---

[1] Or another legal obligation.

then the additional nil-rate band is available to cover the amount of RNRB that has been lost because that residence was no longer part of the estate on the person's death. This downsizing addition is subject to a formal claim by the personal representatives within two years of the end of the month in which a person dies. The downsizing addition is available on one disposal of a former residence only and the method for calculating the amount is set out in IHTA 1984, s. 8FA*ff.*

Law: IHTA 1984, s. 8FA-8FE; FA 2016, s. 93 and Sch. 15

Table of primary legislation

Index of cases

General index

213

Printed and bound in Great Britain by
Marston Book Services Limited, Oxfordshire